The Sound of One Hand Clapping

To my students, and all my teachers

Sheila Yeger

The Sound of One Hand Clapping

A Guide to Writing for the Theatre

AMBER LANE PRESS

Published in 1990 by
Amber Lane Press Ltd.
Church Street
Charlbury, Oxford OX7 3PR

(Tel: 0608 810024)

Typeset in Century Old Style
by Oxonian Rewley Press Ltd., Oxford.

Printed and bound in Great Britain by
Richard Clay Ltd, Bungay, Suffolk

Copyright © Sheila Yeger, 1990

ISBN: 1 872868 02 9

Contents

Acknowledgements

The author and publishers wish to thank the following who have kindly given permission for the use of copyright material:

Caryl Churchill for extracts from *Top Girls* (Methuen Drama); Barrie Keeffe for the extract from *Abide With Me* (Methuen Drama); Steve Gooch for the extract from *Mister Fun* (Metro Theatre Company); Heidi Thomas for the extracts from *Shamrocks and Crocodiles* and *Indigo* (Amber Lane Press).

MASTER: In clapping both hands a sound is heard. What is the sound of the one hand?

ANSWER: The pupil faces his Master, takes a correct posture, and, without a word, thrusts one hand forward.

Zen Koan

I've Always Wanted to Write But . . .

– The workshop process – Overcoming your inhibitions –
– The tools of the trade – A place to work –
– Establishing a routine – Facing the blank sheet of paper –

In 1988 I was invited by Gilly Adams, Artistic Director of the 'Made in Wales' Theatre Company, to run a series of workshops for women who were interested in writing for the theatre.

The idea for these workshops had first taken root at a symposium on women's writing organised by the company in the previous year.

Frustrated at the frequently heard lament of artistic directors— "We'd like to do new work/women's work but we don't get any good plays." — we had spoken of the need to nurture new writing by creating a supportive and stimulating environment in which such work could be brought to fruition. I had suggested that much potentially good work was probably lost because the writer lacked the confidence or the expertise to complete a piece of work without some form of support. "Give me ten women," I had rashly said, "And I'll give you ten plays."

A year later, at the end of the first series of workshops, there were indeed ten plays. Even though one participant had dropped out, another, quite unaware of my boast, had helpfully produced two pieces of work.

The following year I repeated the process with a smaller group. Again, each participant produced a piece of work which, if not yet viable for production, was at least in a form which might be developed to that stage.

More important, perhaps, was the fact that several members of the group, encouraged by the achievement of having actually followed a piece of work through from start to finish to their own satisfaction, were now prepared to take themselves more seriously as writers.

None of this was easy, quick or painless. On the contrary, all the writers involved had to make a very great commitment of time and energy, showing extraordinary courage in their willingness to open up to each other and share what is essentially an intensely private activity.

I would like to make it clear from the outset that this book does not contain any magic, automatic formulas or cast-iron rules. It is not 'playwriting made easy' nor the 'do-it-yourself guide to writing for the theatre', for there can be no such thing. I myself have found no easy answers to the questions all writers must face; I can offer no short cuts or dreams of escape from the sheer hard work, loneliness, boredom and frustration that most writers experience, at least some of the time.

Writing for the theatre is my profession and also my passion. I do it because there is nothing else I would rather do and because I think it is worth doing. Since I believe that the theatre cannot survive without new writing I am committed to helping to develop new work wherever I can. By 'new work' I don't simply mean work that has just been written. I mean work that is radical, original, provocative; work that refuses to accept the status quo but continually breaks new ground; work that, at its very best, is capable of changing people's hearts and minds.

My objective with this book, as with my workshops is, therefore, to be subversive and to challenge received notions about how to write a play or even what to write about. I wish to incite the new writer to be more daring, more innovative, more honest and more passionate.

I hope to do this not by laying down rules to be slavishly followed but by providing a loose framework in which a relatively inexperienced playwright might find both the stimulation and the support to complete a piece of work.

I regard this book as a sharing of experience rather than an academic treatise and so I have tried to avoid theorising in favour of practical suggestions.

The workshops I ran were in the nature of an experiment for me in that I was interested to see whether a flexible and rather tentative approach would prove beneficial to the participants. It was quite a risky way to work, both for the students and myself since I could not hide behind expertise and they did not have the security, however false, of a set of rigid guidelines to follow.

My intention in this book is to reflect the essentially exploratory nature of those workshops and the flexibility with which we worked. Where examples seem useful I often illustrate a point by reference to students' work in progress rather than to a published or performed piece. Sometimes I refer to work later substantially revised or even abandoned. What goes wrong or fails to work is often more revealing, in retrospect, than what comes to fruition.

I also want to share with the reader the doubts, fears and uncertainties experienced by all of those at the workshops (including myself) at various stages of the process because these too are very much a part of being a writer.

The first part of the book is divided into broad topics such as Research; Character and Dialogue; Structure. This is not because any of these subjects can really be dealt with in isolation but because I think it is simpler to focus on each in turn whilst bearing in mind that they are all part of a unified approach to writing in general and writing a play in particular. Each chapter finishes with suggestions or projects, which are designed to give you an opportunity to experiment and try out techniques in a 'safe' situation and to give you more confidence when you start work on the play itself. For those of you who have little or no previous experience of writing, the projects should act both as a stimulus and a gentle introduction to the pains and pleasures which lie ahead.

The second part of the book aims to guide you through the actual writing process, from first draft to the (almost) finished script.

This is followed by some discussion on how your play might be moved closer to production with the help of a director and actors.

Finally, there is some advice on how to market your play once you are satisfied that you have done as much work on it as you can.

******

The 'Made in Wales' workshops were run exclusively for women writers. I make no apology for my partisan interest in women's work and the particular difficulties encountered by women in bringing that work before an audience. Nevertheless, I hope that this book will prove helpful to all those playwrights who are prepared to take the necessary risks involved in writing for the theatre.

Anyone who has ever attended one of my workshops will know that my first words are usually: "Put away your notebooks . . . nobody can teach you to write."

Nobody can teach you to write because you are already a writer. All I can do is to try to help you to confront and overcome the fears, self-doubt and inhibitions which have so far prevented you from expressing yourself fully in writing.

"I've always wanted to write but . . ." Behind the unfinished sentence lies many a story.

▷ "I've always wanted to write but I'm too busy."

▷ "I've always wanted to write but the children need me."

▷ "I've always wanted to write but by the time I get home from work I'm exhausted."

▷ "I've always wanted to write but I can't because of . . . the housework / gardening / decorating / the dog / cat / hamster / my lover / mother / father / husband."

▷ "I've always wanted to write but I haven't got a . . . quiet place to work / typewriter / word processor / publisher / director / agent / copy of the *Writers' and Artists' Yearbook* / clue where to begin."

Perhaps the most important first step for all would-be writers is to confront their own excuses. Of course the obstacles *do* exist; they are real. They present genuine problems. No one would suggest that three toddlers or a tiring and responsible full-time job do not constitute an impediment to the flowering of your creativity. It's all a question of the degree of urgency you feel. If your desire to write has reached boiling point then you will find a way of doing it, however selfish, foolish or calculating it may seem. Nothing and nobody will stop you. But up to that point anything and everything will stand in your way. This is because the real reason you have not yet begun to write is undoubtedly far more complex than you realise. The blocks we put in the way of our own creativity are subtle, individual and insidious. Formed as a result of years of conditioning, of trying to fit into shapes other people have designed for us, they can feel surprisingly concrete and quite immovable.

Perhaps it might be more honest to admit: "I've always wanted to write but . . . I'm afraid that I'll find it all too difficult, go mad, be a total failure, not be able to earn a proper living, look stupid, make people angry, never finish anything."

Don't worry . . . It's really quite normal to be frightened. Indeed, it would be quite unusual *not* to feel fear at this stage. Perhaps you have been dreaming of writing since you were a child. Now, suddenly, you find yourself almost ready to embark on the journey. Soon Pandora's box will spring open and everything will be terrible and wonderful, life-enhancing, overwhelming, totally revolutionary. Your journey will almost certainly lead you away from the safe, the predictable, the structured, the organised, into a landscape which is both utterly familiar and terrifyingly strange. Is it any wonder that you sharpen pencils, tidy drawers, feed the baby, go to the office, clean, cook, mow the lawn, walk the dog, invoke the bank manager — that you invent any excuse, seek any diversion to prevent you having to pick up the pen and actually start WRITING?

Then there's always the problem of equipment. At least you can make it a problem if you'd like to. But you don't need a word processor or even a typewriter in order to write a play. A pencil will do, and a sheet of paper; even the back of an old envelope is good enough for making a few notes. Forget technology at present. Expensive computers may boost your self-esteem but they can also become dangerous toys, lending a false authority and spurious finality to work still very much in progress. What is in your imagination is what's important at present, not what sits gleaming on your desk. I speak as a total Luddite who can't even type, but pen on paper is still, for me, the real act of writing, where it all begins.

A notebook, however, *is* a useful tool of the trade, something to carry with you wherever you go. You might use it to record impressions, snatches of 'found' dialogue: all playwrights must learn to be shameless eavesdroppers. Don't censor your note-taking or attempt to categorise these random jottings in any way. Don't be neat and tidy, systematic or organised. This notebook is for your eyes only; you are not going to have to read chunks of it aloud to an audience, show it to anyone or have to account for it in any way. It is your first real luxury, a total self-indulgence. It will make you feel more like a writer than half a dozen word processors.

A quiet place to work is probably helpful, though I know of at least one prolific writer who does much of his work on trains, in pubs, sports-centres, or on his knee whilst watching the six o'clock news. I, on the other hand, can hardly write a serious word unless there is total silence. Even a bird singing in the wrong key can induce total mental paralysis.

A place where you regularly work may actually help you to get started. You are trying to take yourself seriously as a writer, someone whose work it is to put words on paper. It doesn't have to be an office or even a library. If you find it easiest to write in the bath, then write there . . .

New writers often ask me how many hours a day or week they should write. The answer is . . . don't say 'should'. It's probably better to establish a realistic work routine of just one hour a day than to set yourself an impossible goal which you then fail to achieve. One of my students was concerned about her slow progress on her workshop play. She had two young children and could 'only' manage to work about seven hours a day. She felt tired and frustrated and wondered if she would ever finish the play. She was surprised when I cautiously suggested that perhaps she was doing too much, that she might be more genuinely productive if she went for a walk by the river, stopped to look at trees, did nothing at all . . . in fact anything to relieve some of the pressure she was placing on herself by the fierce and unrealistic regime she had devised.

Every writer will find the work pattern which suits her best. One writer can be very happy working for a leisurely two hours every morning; another will prefer to work flat out all night and sleep all day. It depends on circumstances, energy, personality, personal preference, and what priority you feel you want or need to give to your writing at this time. What ends up on paper is, anyway, only the exposed tip of the iceberg. What goes on when you're not writing is probably just as important, perhaps more so. Sometimes, sitting looking out at the view can prove unexpectedly productive, so can going for a swim or making some soup. Whilst the blank page can appear incredibly hostile and unforgiving, the subterranean process must be trusted and allowed to work in its own way.

Deciding to write a play is, in itself, a proclamation of anarchy, a distinct and deliberate move away from most accepted norms of behaviour. You, an adult, are about to give yourself licence to speak in imaginary voices, to invent imaginary places, to move people about in your make-believe world as if they were counters in a game of Monopoly. You are a magician with a box of tricks, a storyteller who doesn't necessarily know the end of the story till you get there.

It's a mysterious business and it is probably a mistake to expect anyone (with the possible exception of another writer) to respect, understand or sympathise with the process. That's why, if you insist on rules, I am inclined to suggest only these.

▷ **Don't talk about it**

> Do it. The more people you tell, the less need you will have to write the story. You will only write when you feel that there is no alternative. When a friend asks what you are going to write about, the best answer is: "I'm waiting to find out."

▷ **Never apologise**

> Being a writer is learning, slowly and painfully, to speak your own truth, to trust your own distinctive voice, to dare to shape the world in the way you want to see it, and to communicate what you see to your audience or reader. At first this will all seem very unfamiliar, risky and presumptious. Later you will feel that it is the most natural thing to do. But it's a difficult transition to make and it takes time and a certain amount of daring.

You've always *wanted* to write but up to now you've allowed circumstances, people, your own perfectly realistic fears and misgivings to get in the way. Now, perhaps, you are ready . . .

CHAPTER ONE

Writing for the Theatre

– Why the theatre? – Telling the story –
– The essence of drama – Writing for an audience –
– Theatre as communal experience – Craft and inspiration –
– Theatre as magic –

Since this is intended to be a practical book I'll assume that you have already decided that you would like to write a play and are looking for some advice on how to go about it.

If I were to embark, at this stage, on an academic discussion of the many theories concerning theatre or a detailed analysis of the various attitudes, practices and philosophies to be found in theatre today, you might feel reassuringly well-informed but I doubt that it would actually result in your writing a single word. It's all too easy to convince yourself that *thinking* about writing is the same as writing itself and that research into the theory of the thing will somehow reduce the need to put pen to paper.

Nor does this seem an appropriate place to enter into a heated argument concerning the lack of adequate state funding, which threatens to starve theatre at its very source and make playwrights, as described in a recent Theatre Writers' Union publication, an "endangered species".

I shall take it for granted that you have a burning passion to write a play, a passion so intense that no practical consideration could begin to deter you, and that your starting point is a fierce commitment to live theatre and a powerful desire to communicate your particular vision of the universe to an audience.

Unless you feel as strongly as this I think I ought to advise you to look for another form of expression since, in deciding to write for the theatre, you are undoubtedly presenting yourself with an awesome challenge.

Perhaps you are already losing patience with all this talk of passion and commitment. Theatre is a form of entertainment and surely it can't be *so* difficult to imitate any of the totally uncontroversial and anodyne experiences to be had in any of a dozen theatres across the land.

It would be quite wrong for me to offer even the most rudimentary suggestions on how you might begin to write a play without stating my own view of what theatre is and what part is played by the playwright in bringing a play before an audience.

You have all been to the theatre once or twice, or maybe many times. You have sat in plush seats before crimson curtains, applauded lavish designs and magnificent costumes. You have shivered in draughty church halls with windows that rattle and scenery that wobbles, or worse. You have been moved to tears in a room above a pub with the noise of glasses clinking below, or bored to death in an illustrious and glossy temple dedicated to the 'art' of theatre. Or vice versa. You have watched plays that are good, plays that are bad and plays that are unspeakably awful. You have seen plays which seem technically perfect but which somehow feel spiritually bankrupt and plays that are blatantly without shape or structure but are nevertheless startlingly powerful. You have admired performances, or music or sets, or laughed when the scenery fell down. You have been amazed, baffled, enraged, uplifted, overwhelmed, irritated. Sometimes all at once. Occasionally, you will have been able to say exactly how the play had that effect on you; more often your reaction will have been quite beyond words.

Perhaps you have made an academic study of the texts of 'great' writers: Shakespeare, Ibsen, Chekhov, the Greeks. You may have acquainted yourself with a number of facts concerning the history of theatre. If so, you will already have formed an opinion about whether you regard theatre as a form of escape or as a mirror held up to life, an instrument of change or a faithful portrait of things as they are. You may even have decided that you intend to write a play that is naturalistic or surreal, comic or tragic.

Or perhaps it is a great deal simpler than that. You have a story to tell, something you have been carrying around in your head for a while; now it is gradually coming to boiling point, demanding to be told. Could it be a play?

I can't imagine why anyone would decide to write a play, as opposed to a story, a poem or a novel, unless they had already experienced as spectator, or possibly actor, the extraordinary power of theatre, unless they had been part of an audience and become involved in that unique transaction, where the actors agree to pretend to be these people, say these things, do these things, if the audience will agree to believe in them totally.

I think that I decided that I wanted to write plays on the night I saw Tutte Lemkow perform Kafka's *Lecture to an Academy.*

The audience sat in the fully lit small auditorium. On the platform which served as a stage there was a lectern . . . nothing else. We waited. Nothing happened. The lights did not go down; there was no music. Suddenly we became aware of a scratching noise outside the main door. It sounded like an animal asking to be let in. The door opened and we saw a gorilla dressed in a dinner jacket and holding the notes from which he was to lecture to us. Of course we knew, as rational adults, that this must be an actor impersonating a gorilla but such was the power of the text he was to deliver, and the authenticity of his observation and portrayal of gorilla-behaviour, that we willingly agreed to be convinced. Till, at the end of the piece, when the apparently 'civilised' creature began to chew on his notes and lollop gorilla-fashion around the auditorium, the screams of the audience were real enough. Had we been watching a man pretending to be a gorilla, or a gorilla pretending to be a man, or both? Perhaps the answer was irrelevant. What mattered more is that we had all been involved in a strange and terrifying event — an experience which had forced us to abandon our objectivity and carefully preserved self-control and respond instinctively and without constraint to the combined power of both word and performance.

Moments like this in the theatre are seminal and sadly all too infrequent. I can still remember the closing sequences of *An die Musik*, the astonishing and shocking play about prisoners in a concentration camp performed by the Pip Simmons group at the I.C.A. in London in the 1960's.

Although I can't recall one word of the actual text, the emotion aroused in me by the occasion is still somehow present and potent. I can still draw on it, refer to it; it has become a part of my inner vocabulary.

Similarly, I can still see a cornfield growing onto the stage, and a man in love with a pig in Caryl Churchill's remarkable and evocative *A Mouthful of Birds*. I can recall how much these images moved and startled me, even though the exact context may have faded from memory.

Yet, in all the instances quoted above, what I have referred to is not a specific text but a total experience of theatre. I can't remember the words at all; what I remember is the moment, the emotions I felt. How much of that experience came from what the writer had written, how much from the actors' skills, the designer's imagination or the director's insight, and how much from the sensation of sharing all this with a roomful of strangers, I cannot say, nor does it seem particularly relevant. What I do know is that I sat in an audience and was deeply affected by what I saw and heard. It was the result of a creative collaboration and it demanded my reaction to complete the process.

These are two major factors, therefore, that set writing for the theatre apart from other forms of creative expression. The first is the essentially co-operative nature of the process and the second is the need for an audience.

Though a play tells the writer's story and conveys a particular vision of the world, it only works properly when the actors and director lift it off the page and give it three-dimensional life. The audience too is essential — a random collection of individuals, who come together in an experience which is both communal and very intimate.

When everyday events strike us as so naturally dramatic, entertaining or poignant that we describe them as 'pure theatre', we are alluding not to the mechanics but to the quality of the experience itself.

An old lady has got onto the wrong train and immediately involves her fellow passengers in a crisis. This is theatre.

An argument breaks out at the supermarket over who is first in the queue; somebody shouts, laughs, bursts into tears. This is theatre.

At the Social Security office, a young mother threatens to abandon her baby unless financial help is forthcoming. This too is theatre.

We have all seen and read too many plays which lack this essential richness and vitality: the sense of crisis, risk and resolution; the feast for the eye, ear and mind. The would-be playwright can learn a great deal from considering what is so powerful in the incidents described above — what elements they contain which fire the imagination, demand attention, evoke emotion, ensure response.

▷ **Jerzy Grotowski** defined theatre as:
  "What takes place between spectator and actor."

▷ **Peter Brook** wrote:
  "I can take any empty space and call it a bare stage. A man walks
  across this empty space whilst someone else is watching and that
  is all that is needed for an act of theatre to be engaged."

Both of these definitions or thoughts on the nature of theatre were suggested by directors, which means that I offer them to you by way of direct provocation. I think they will encourage you to be very basic and rigorous with yourself from the start.

In deciding to write a play, as opposed to a novel or short story, by choosing that particular form to convey your ideas, you are stepping out of whatever ivory tower you may have inhabited into a bustling and often terrifying arena. That's why I must encourage you to be both practical and philosophical as you begin to consider what a play is and what function you as a playwright might be expected to fulfil in relation to the other practitioners who help to make theatre happen.

I am no proponent of theatre without text but I believe it would be cruel to allow you to embark on your play with the mistaken idea that every word you write will automatically be sacrosanct, that what you conceive of in your imagination can necessarily be translated exactly as it stands into three dimensions and offered to an audience.

On the contrary, at every stage in the process, your text will have to work hard to be recognised, will have to fight for its survival. It will be subjected to every form of analysis, scrutiny and questioning by director, actors and, finally, audience. What seemed perfectly clear to you in your imagination must seem equally clear to an audience who have not been able to follow your thought processes. Remember: they won't be able to turn back the pages, like the reader of a novel who has failed to grasp something. Nor will you be there to guide their response, like a poet reading your own work aloud.

If you are a woman writer you will face the particular challenge of depicting a view which may seem alien and unfamiliar to almost all who encounter it. You will have to contend with directors, actors and subsequently audiences whose responses are subtly tuned to a male analysis and who will find it hard, if not impossible, to accord validity to your viewpoint.

The implication of all this seems to be that you must be quite clear in your own mind right from the start what you intend to say and how you hope to say it. Flexibility will, of course, be demanded of you at a later stage. What is needed at the beginning is a very strong sense of your own intentions, a clarity of vision, and a determination to use all means at your disposal to be as specific as you can.

Sometimes new playwrights will explain a gap in the text by saying: "I've left that up to the director" or will justify some vagueness in dialogue or characterisation by suggesting that the actor can decide for himself what something means or how it fits into the overall whole. This is a dangerous practice and can have disastrous results.

Though it's important for the text of a new play to remain fluid while the director, actors and designer pool their imaginations to lift it from the page, it is equally important for the writer to be very specific and focussed about her intentions at every stage of the process.

In an ideal situation, writer and director are mutually interdependent, the work of one feeding and complementing the work of the other, both active and equal partners in a creative collaboration.

In the real world of all too scarce resources the writer, particularly the inexperienced writer, is often forced into the role of humble supplicant, vying with many others to gain the attention of one busy director.

Yet, when the relationship works well, there is enormous potential for a dynamic interaction which can result in very exciting theatre.

I am fortunate enough to enjoy such a fruitful relationship with the gifted director, Annie Castledine, who commissioned my play *Self Portrait* and effectively nursed it through to completion. Mutual trust, a certain outspokenness on her part, and a free interchange of ideas, resulted in the play developing far beyond its original, more timid conception. Our artistic collaboration enabled me, as the writer, to make more daring leaps of the imagination than I might otherwise have felt possible.

Throughout this process, however, the essential vision is still, and should be, that of the writer. The story is, after all, the writer's story; the characters are drawn from the writer's imagination or memory. None of this has any life before you call it into existence. What finally happens on the stage is, in the best circumstances, firmly rooted in what you imagined in the first instance, containing the very essence of what you had hoped to communicate, even though what the audience actually experiences is a result of the unique fusion of the creative energies of many people.

Bringing a play to production is a very delicate procedure, fraught with difficulty for the writer. Yet I must assume that if you intend to write a play it's because you would like to see it performed. It is vital that you understand the process which will lead to this and are prepared to enter into it.

Although this may all seem rather daunting it's as well to be very clear about it from the start. If you don't think you will be able to subject yourself or your work to this process then it might be better to stick to writing novels, poetry or articles. Writing for the theatre demands an extraordinary confidence in the validity of your own voice combined with the flexibility to let go of your work in order to allow the creative process to continue. Achieving the fine balance between preserving your individual vision and being able to open up to the imagination of others is one of the most difficult things you must learn to do as a playwright.

The prospect of writing a play is always enormously exciting, containing the promise of a rich and complex experience. At the beginning of each new piece of work I sense the same mixture of terror and elation, the same overwhelming desire to create and enter a strange imaginary world, the same fear of what I might find there.

You, the playwright, can be both craftsman and magician, a Prospero of the written word, conjuring up images where none existed before, creating living beings out of thin air.

You are not primarily a recorder of the truth (whatever that might be), a historian or a reporter, though at times you may be all of these. You are, instead, an extremely selective and partisan storyteller, working with actors and director to make something happen which will affect the audience in a very specific and calculated way.

The audience is always the unknown factor. Until you watch your first play you have no real idea of what you have written or its potential to shock, move or change the perceptions of those who watch it. But, as a playwright, you can't afford to ignore the part played by the audience. Whatever you want to say or show must come to life with sufficient authenticity to encourage them to permit the 'willing suspension of disbelief' that is an essential component of their experience.

Even in the theatre of Brecht, who, in deference to his audience, preferred actively to remind them that they were only watching a play, and who employed various devices to keep the audience aware that these were actors, not real people, we are still invited to enter a rich world of invention and fantasy.

I sat recently in a large and noisy audience at the Berliner Ensemble, the theatre created by Brecht in East Berlin. There was very little artificial barrier between the performers and a crowd who seemed delightfully familiar with both the resident company and *Baal*, the play which forms part of its regular repertoire. Yet, such was the power of the text and the ideas it conveyed, that we were quickly caught up in the fortunes of the protagonist, living with him through the humorous and painful experiences depicted on the stage. However much Brecht reminded us that what we were watching was not 'real life', we were still happily absorbed into the fantasy.

Theatre is, after all, one of our last surviving communal experiences, which is perhaps why audiences, starved of spectacle, ritual, passion and poetry will hungrily devour all of these if you can only offer them the opportunity.

Television, mostly viewed in solitude, or with one or two companions, accompanied always by the trivial music of domestic pursuits, evoking instant comment or inevitable interruption, lacks both the intimacy and the sense of occasion of the theatre.

In the theatre nothing is ever 'too much' for an audience, though I'm all too frequently aware that what is being offered is far too little. It's not a question of scale but of intensity, a willingness to take enormous risks without fear of the consequences.

I have seen the same quality of response in an audience watching *To*, a tight two-hander by Jim Cartwright at the Octagon Theatre in Bolton, as in the audience which mingled with the cast of one hundred and fifty at a performance of *The Western Women*, a community play by Ann Jellicoe at Lyme Regis in Dorset. What was happening in each case was that the audience had completely lost their inhibitions. The play had persuaded them to open up, to lower their usual barriers, to laugh, cry, or join in the singing without constraint, to be ready to break the rules or change their minds.

This is not a question of complicated techniques that are beyond the novice but rather a sort of fierce clarity which derives from the writer's ability to be very honest about his/her intentions. In *To* Cartwright makes no bones about the fact that he means to explode myths about masculinity. He does so with a skilful mixture of compassion and humour which leaves the spectators with little choice but to abandon their defences and consider the possibilities laid before them with their minds perhaps more open than usual.

Similarly, in *The Western Women,* Jellicoe is not afraid to make a blatant appeal to the emotions; if the techniques of both script and performance are apparently unsophisticated they are nevertheless deployed with a shrewd awareness of how an audience might react in given circumstances, and so are hugely effective.

The first criterion for me of whether a play is working or not is to try to hear the actors speaking the lines to an audience and to imagine that audience responding.

However beautiful or accomplished a play may look on the printed page it can only work in three dimensions: that is its prime function and its purpose. That's why, from the outset, it's important to think of your play in terms of 'theatre' rather than words on a page, to attempt to visualise the functioning whole rather than its individual parts.

That's not to say that there is no room for poetry, description or imagery in dramatic writing; indeed, there is a positive requirement to see them used. What you write must speak to an audience and the characters you create must achieve a reality beyond the mere ideas. Without this you may find that what you have written is powerful but not dramatic, static rather than alive with action, that it describes rather than demonstrates events. You may have produced a fine piece of writing but will it function as a play?

I don't intend to dwell on the state of theatre and on the question of financial restraints imposed by scarce resources. Yet I can't altogether neglect this subject since it obviously has a serious bearing on what may, or may not, happen to your play once it is written.

The kind of theatre we are beginning to talk about is not necessarily the kind to meet with the instant approval of those who prefer a quiet life. It is potentially subversive, possibly disruptive and full of all kinds of exciting and dangerous possibilities. My intention is to encourage you to give full rein to your imagination in all its glorious potential without paying undue attention to practical considerations. Nevertheless, it would be irresponsible to suggest that, in the current economic climate, a play with a cast of twenty stands as good a chance as one with a cast of two; or that, if a play is overtly provocative in subject matter it will be a popular choice with artistic directors concerned about sponsorship or state funding.

If this book were entitled *Writing for Pleasure and Profit* I would consider it my brief to offer you a blueprint for the kind of play most likely to win you fame and fortune. Perhaps there is a formula which, if followed to the letter, can only result in West End success and a healthy bank balance.

If there is such a formula I have never discovered it, but to be honest, I have spent very little time looking for it. Instead, I have regarded each new piece of work as a puzzle to be solved, a journey to be embarked upon, usually without a map. Sometimes the puzzle has proved too complex to yield any satisfactory solution; sometimes the journey has taken me to places I might rather have left unvisited.

I have also tried, with varying degrees of success, to earn a living by writing for the theatre, which means, at the end of this journey, I have usually offered the results of my work to a director asking her/him to decide whether an audience could be expected to watch, understand and respond to what I have written.

By a slow and painful process of trial by experience I have begun to learn a little more of what might and what might not work in a theatre. I have learnt that I can be disastrously wrong in my estimation of how an audience will respond; I have also learnt that occasionally my own instincts are right. Sometimes other people, apparently more expert than I, have rejected a play, or failed to understand my intentions, when an audience has responded from the very gut with a depth and spontaneity none of us had envisaged.

That is why, when students ask me whether what they see in their mind's eye, what they sense in their deepest imaginings, can actually be achieved in theatrical terms, can be communicated to an audience, I know that there is no easy answer. The most important thing is to be honest to yourself, to say what you feel must and should be said, and to hope that the power of your convictions will carry the audience with you.

Of course, inspiration alone won't write a play but it will set the wheels in motion. You will still need to learn your craft as much as if you were a painter, a potter or a silversmith. No artist can achieve the desired results without some experience of the raw materials and without some practice at using them to their best advantage. Skills have to be developed.

I suppose that writing anything is a strange mixture of pure inspiration and sheer hard work. The theatre has the added dimension of being a medium which makes certain specific practical demands on the writer.

The craft of writing a play can be worked on, developed and refined but the initial inspiration which has made you want to write at all has an altogether more mysterious and fragile quality.

For the purpose of this book I am assuming that, as a playwright, you are a virtual beginner, but that some sense of the magic of theatre has attracted or excited you sufficiently to want to communicate with an audience.

Perhaps you have already tried to write a play but have abandoned the attempt. Perhaps you did finish something only to have it rejected by a director or management.

I would like to try to harness the enthusiasm, indeed passion, which first inspired you to think that writing for the theatre might be a challenge, and to try to help you to develop some basic skills to enable you to write more effectively and more powerfully in that medium.

I know that the actual nuts and bolts of writing plays can be daunting. Questions concerning the use of stage directions, the mechanics of moving characters from place to place, accents and dialect can prove a very real stumbling block in the early stages of conceiving a play. However, if these are confronted without panic they often prove far less problematic than appeared at first.

My work with women writers has made me very conscious of the particular problems which they experience as they consider the possibility of writing for the theatre.

As well as suffering from every writer's fears of appearing foolish, of being unable to translate into words what seems so clear in the imagination, the woman playwright is assailed by numerous other crises of confidence.

Surrounded by predominantly male role models and conscious of the fact that her play, when completed, cannot fail to offer that all too rare analysis of the world — a female viewpoint — it is particularly difficult for a woman to dare to speak in her own authentic voice. Timidity and fear hamper women writers in every sphere but nowhere more than in the world of the theatre.

I think that is why women find a group setting supportive and endorsing and why, in this safe environment, they feel able to write freely. In my workshops women have produced work that has moved and excited me by its daring, its honesty and its clarity. However, this book is for all writers who are prepared to open up to new possibilities in themselves and in their work, to challenge their own preconceptions and those of their prospective audience, to expose themselves perhaps to criticism, incomprehension or ridicule.

I have no interest in the kind of theatre which flatters and endorses the cosy assumptions of a narrow band of society, which panders to prejudice and stereotype, whether it be racial, sexual, social or psychological.

The theatre I am interested in looks critically at the relationship between an individual and society and actively suggests the possibility of change.

I hope for a theatre that challenges the accepted norms, and provokes, disturbs, undermines — one that destroys preconceptions and exposes complacency.

Theatre is a powerful though often underrated force for change in both the individual and society. It also provides a rare and precious opportunity for a rich communal experience, a chance to introduce ritual, symbol, romance, colour, music, poetry and passion into everyday life.

If theatre is a kind of magic then you, the playwright, are the magician. That is why I hope that you will be very daring, and very passionate, in your approach and that, however modest the scale of your first play, you will begin to explore in it all the infinite possibilities of writing in this most challenging medium.

CHAPTER TWO

The Raw Material

– Exploring a memory – Choosing a subject –
– Finding the real subject – Working from experience –
– Writing an autobiographical play – Eavesdropping –
– The biographical subject – Historical events –
– Community plays – Developing a theme –
– The female viewpoint –
– **Project: Activating your imagination** –

It is unusual for someone to say: "What shall I write?" Most writers, however inexperienced, feel that they have a story to tell or an idea they would like to communicate. More often I am asked: "Can I *really* write about that?" (ie: am I *allowed* to?). Or, more specifically: "Surely that's not the sort of thing I could put into a play?"

In both instances, the underlying assumption is that certain things are 'suitable' subject matter and others are not, that certain events/characters/issues are worthy of dramatic treatment and others are too trivial or personal to qualify.

That's why, at my first workshop session, I refused to ask the students what they hoped to write about. At this stage this would only have produced what is essentially a 'dutiful' response: students would have offered me a subject that seemed to fulfil what they imagined to be the accepted criteria. What they thought was suitable would have depended on a variety of factors involving a subtle and insidious set of self-censoring devices which they had subconsciously learnt to apply. For example, a 'suitable' subject for a writer who has been through a long formal education may be one which sounds very erudite and academic and will undoubtedly require a great deal of factual research. Perhaps it will concern a figure in history or a well-documented historical event.

Another writer, eager to show evidence of her political affiliations, may suggest a subject that is designed to explore some social injustice or reveal concern about the circumstances of certain individuals or groups.

These subjects have certain things in common. They sound important and very 'objective'. They would be promising material for a thesis or an article in a scholarly journal. There's no reason at all why they should not form a perfectly good basis for a play, were it not for the fact that they are often not what the writer really wants to write about. This is her 'official' subject, the one she offers up for approval. At this stage she may be quite convinced that she will write the exact play she describes. Yet her real subject is yet to be revealed.

So, instead, I'll ask you, as I asked my students in the workshop, to search for a memory, something which feels particularly potent, very personal, a memory which haunts and obsesses.

This isn't because I think that these memories will necessarily, or in any direct way, form the basis of the play you are eventually to write, but because I feel that it is vital from the outset to activate that part of the consciousness normally held in check, left unexplored or subdued, and to locate it as a source of inspiration and energy. I also feel that you need, even at this early stage, to connect with the sense of risk, the possibility of entering deep waters, which seems an essential ingredient of all creative activity. I don't want you to feel too secure, too sure of the process, too eager to fall back on old methods, on tried and tested techniques. This is to be an altogether different kind of experience.

Pat Lewis's response to my challenge in the workshop was to write an extremely detailed description of the kitchen of the house she lived in as a child. It is poor, shabby, dominated by her father's possessions which neither she nor her mother are allowed to touch: his fishing tackle, a stuffed wild duck. She remembers these objects as frightening to a child, while admitting that in retrospect the scene seems colourful, even romantic. And on the table she sees a peeled orange. Yes, it's definitely peeled. So extraordinarily specific is her memory of the scene, the events which occurred there fresh and accessible as though they had happened yesterday. For this memory is Pat's obsession; it has been haunting her all through her adult life. When she reads us the description in all its vivid detail, we know instinctively that this is her *real* subject, that whatever form she chooses, she will be impelled to explore this memory and what it means.

John Berger writes in an essay on the sculptor Henry Moore: "We are talking about obsessions which determine the gestures and perceptions of artists throughout a life's work, even when their conscious attention is elsewhere. A kind of bias of the imagination. The way a life slips towards a theme which is home to that writer."

It is this 'bias of the imagination' which leads a writer to a particular starting-point, which causes her to choose *this* rather than *that* way of dealing with what she sees, hears or experiences. It is an unconscious process of selection, which is going on beneath the surface at all times and which colours everything.

Two people witnessing the same event will each perceive it through the filter of their own preconceptions. If you ask them to give an account of what they saw, their 'objective' description of events will be biased by their particular prejudices, philosophies, life experiences, and emotional state. Guided by their individual obsession they will focus, probably quite unconsciously, on those aspects of the story which most effectively feed that obsession.

For example, let me tell you about a surprise party given for a 65-year-old friend. Part of the surprise is a 'strippogram' in the shape of a young girl dressed as a rather provocative policewoman. She takes off her uniform to reveal a shabby black chemise. She dances listlessly with her 'client'. Her stiletto heels are broken down, her eyes are expressionless, her hair is lank and not very clean. I am reminded of the 'Ten cents a dance' girls of the American depression and the dance marathons, where desperate people danced themselves literally to death in the hope of a cash prize. I watch the faces of the other guests, middle-class, middle-aged and mostly affluent. They look on with a mixture of vicarious pleasure, memories of other days, a little mild, containable shock. Suddenly, surprisingly, she kisses her 'client' quite tenderly on the cheek; perhaps he reminds her of her father . . . ?

This is, of course, only how I tell the story. Ask anyone present and you will get quite a different account. It's obviously far from objective since, even without any intention to do so, I have coloured events with the wash of my own prejudices, and my own personal preoccupations, which must be instantly apparent to the reader.

Pat V. T. West discusses the genesis of her play *Babylon*, in which the story of a woman 'invaded' by a group of builders becomes a metaphor for the position of women in a patriarchal society.

She describes how the builders took over the top-floor flat where she lives alone with her young son. "There they all were in my life and I was forced to live with men for months when my whole life is about *not* living with men. There they all were, climbing in and out of my windows and so on. Yet they themselves represented a creative process: they seemed to typify the destruction and upheaval that creative process embodies. The work was something you wanted done: you had to recognise there *is* a male aspect — how the animus works . . ."

To another writer the arrival of builders would have been a minor inconvenience, or a welcome diversion, or even a springboard for broad farce or situation comedy, but to this particular writer their presence acted as a catalyst, activating material already available to her, suggesting a form for ideas already present in her consciousness.

Her response to the stimulus was affected by many things: her past experiences, her understanding, both intellectual and instinctive, of the situation, her emotional and economic state . . . all these factors generated a very specific reaction and resulted in a piece of work which expresses that reaction in dramatic form.

In this broad sense everything you write will be autobiographical. Your work will relate to and derive from your own biography, which predisposes you to experience and interpret events in a very specific way.

At a recent workshop for playwrights organised at the Octagon Theatre in Bolton we were challenged to discover new and more exciting avenues to explore in our attempts to write for the theatre.

One group, under the leadership of Rony Robinson, decided to work overtly with their own autobiographies, revealing and sharing key events in their lives with a view to creating a patchwork of experience which could eventually be shaped and offered to an audience. Though I was not present to see the outcome of this idea I did applaud their open acknowledgement of their own biographies as a rich potential source of inspiration. Judging by the high level of involvement displayed by the group when describing their work process it seemed that they had been both excited and energised by these explorations and were eager to develop the raw material they had discovered, irrespective of the risks involved.

Your own life story is obviously too valuable a source of inspiration to ignore but, whether you are prepared to acknowlege its power or not, it will find its way into your work, with or without your conscious 'permission'.

After All These Years, one of my first stage plays, is about a school reunion. The characters, who were all women, were fictional. None of them was, as far as I knew, based on a real person. I had never, at that point, attended such a reunion, though I had heard a story about a woman who did, and was killed in a car accident on her way home. This I took to be my stimulus. The play dealt with our memories of school, of friendships which emerge as more coercive than supportive, with the interplay of relationships and their effect in later life. It dealt with snobbery, prejudice and bullying, with unfulfilled aspirations, with the great gap between the dream and its fulfilment.

During the long writing of it — three drafts took almost three years — I remembered and relived my time spent as a Jewish scholarship girl at a very staid girls' school, how victimised and excluded I had felt. Yet still I believed I was writing about something I had invented.

At one performance, a friend offered a shrewd comment: "Of course, it's quite obvious that you are *all* the characters. Each one of them expresses a different aspect of you." The play, ostensibly fictional, or perhaps fiction loosely based on fact, was totally, and quite unconsciously autobiographical, a personal journey through very perilous waters.

Perhaps this is where I should sound a note of caution. It's actually quite dangerous to assume that an undiluted blow-by-blow account of events in your own life will automatically prove either fascinating or poignant to your audience. Unless you can find a way of extrapolating from those events the audience may in fact fail to find them of any particular significance. But if what they see and hear resonates with their own memories and experiences they will be prepared to accompany you on your journey.

To return to Pat Lewis's childhood memory of the room and all the specific objects in it, which she described so powerfully. So vivid and precise was her evocation of the scene that each one of us quickly found echoes from our own childhood, memories which hooked us into the drama inherent there and made us hungry to see events unfold.

Iron Them Dry, the play Pat went on to write, was overtly and unashamedly autobiographical in that it depicted incidents and people almost exactly as she remembered them. Yet the story, particular as it was, had a strong resonance for all who had grown up in poor surroundings and fought to escape, who had witnessed their mother's battle to survive against often impossible odds, had fallen in love with the wrong (or even the right) person, or had been embroiled in that most primitive struggle to both express love to and proclaim autonomy from a dominating and undemonstrative father.

The great strength of Pat's story was that, while it was remarkably personal, it was also extremely recognisable, and could therefore work for many people on different levels.

Yet what really convinced me of its potential as raw material for this writer was the passion and courage with which she first shared that memory with us, making little attempt to protect herself in a group of virtual strangers. The subject was so important to her and so ready to be explored that she was prepared to take any risks. I was not surprised when she wrote the first draft at incredible speed; she had been waiting a long time to put those words on paper.

Overt use of autobiographical material characterises the work of many writers. Arnold Wesker, for example, in *Chicken Soup With Barley*, draws on vivid memories of an East End background and real events which took place in the 1930's and involved his own family. The rich characters he creates are closely based on real people.

Although he is not afraid to acknowledge the source of his inspiration, he has subjected his autobiographical material to a careful process of selection. Events have been ordered and juxtaposed so as to give them as much dramatic force as possible. Whilst much of the dialogue may originate in real words uttered at one time or another by real people, he does not have to reproduce their speech line for line, nor does he need to describe the settings brick by brick in order to appear authentic. What he has actually done is to organise the material in a very calculated way so as to achieve a specific effect.

His first intention is to communicate certain ideas to his audience. The material he has available to him from his autobiography is therefore pressed into service, sorted and arranged so as to serve his purpose.

It's quite difficult for the inexperienced writer to work with autobiographical material, even though it may be what she most passionately wants to do. It's hard to decide what to use and what to reject, to discover how to tell the truth, as you see it, without presenting the audience with an indigestible mass of unsifted material. It's often impossible to differentiate between material that is of particular significance to you personally but no one else and material that may be of great relevance to others.

A young writer I had never met sent me a finished play, several hundred pages long, which related, with astonishing attention to factual detail, a series of painful events which had occurred when she and her husband were homeless and living in bed and breakfast accommodation.

As a chronicle of the humiliation and suffering experienced by the unfortunate victims of a harsh and unfeeling system it could not have been more powerful. As a play it didn't work at all. The writer had not felt able to select or rearrange events in any way. What had been important to her was to give a minutely detailed account: the *exact* measurements of an inadequate room, the *specific* words spoken, the *precise* sequence of events which had occurred on a particular day. The result was like a diary. It was not realistic but it was *real*. But there was no art in it; the raw material had not been shaped in any way. As a piece of writing it was extremely informative but oddly monotonous (as, no doubt, were the days and hours it described). It had a tremendous power to educate but not, strangely enough, to move.

I was faced with a dilemma. I could advise the writer how to rearrange what she'd written in order to maximise the dramatic potential or, whilst respecting her need to chronicle these events, I could suggest that they did not, at least in their present form, look like promising material for a play.

So strong was the obvious potential of the material, so tempted was I by the possibility of bringing these matters to the attention of an audience, that I opted for the former approach. I wrote back, offering what I hoped were constructive suggestions as to how she might shape and edit the raw material so as to make it more dramatic.

It was, in the event, quite the wrong decision. What was important to this writer was to bear witness to what had happened to her and to record, in painstaking detail, exactly what she had suffered. To alter any aspect of this record would have proved too difficult to contemplate. I think she found considerable satisfaction in the act of writing everything down. Perhaps it was even valuable to show it to one other person. Eventually she decided that she would take it no further. It had fulfilled its purpose.

People at parties (and elsewhere) often ask: "Where *do* you get your ideas?" The answer is anywhere, everywhere and sometimes nowhere. The writer needs to keep eyes and ears open, to be very receptive to what's going on or what is 'in the air'. Curiosity is essential to any writer, so is a refusal to accept things at their face value.

Eavesdropping is the playwright's stock in trade, the source of much 'found' dialogue, the overhead comment rich with meaning, the apparently innocuous remark which suddenly opens up a whole range of outrageous possibilities to the listener.

There is no need to travel to distant places to find strange and stimulating sights.

I am walking through Waterloo Station when I come across a number of people standing in a circle and speaking to each other in sign language. One of them wears rollers under her scarf.

Their conversation is heated; clearly an argument is in progress. I have no need to know the facts, since I am a playwright, not a reporter. What I see with my eyes is enough to spark off my imagination. Like the incident of the strippogram, what I see immediately merges with what I already carry in my conscious and subconscious mind, and in my heart. My personal bias quite automatically selects aspects of the material and begins, even at this very early stage, to make it distinctively mine.

Even as this process begins, however, it's important to resist a natural desire to impose form onto your new material. Of course it will feel much safer if you can categorise it, if you can begin to marshal it ready for use but, like attempting to bake unproved dough, it is a premature move. The raw material needs time to ripen, without too much conscious intervention on your part. Difficult though it will seem at first, you must learn to leave it alone.

Ideas emerge in some recognisable shape by a mysterious alchemical process that has little to do with logic or intellect. One stimulus reacts with another. Something heard in one place merges with something seen in another. Something you read years ago clicks into place with something you overhear on a bus. You walk in the park and see a group of people: something there reminds you of something else in some other place, at some other time. The permutations are infinite; it's rarely possible to chart the exact point at which your thoughts moved in a particular direction. Ideas are in the wind too and if you allow yourself to be receptive, if you listen with your intuition, you will be instinctively drawn to them as a source of inspiration. The novelist Alice Walker describes this as "keeping the channels open". But this receptivity depends both on your courage and a determination not to seize the first idea which springs to mind, but to wait, watch, listen, respond.

I see the process as a little like the making of a nourishing soup. You have a rich basic stock that's been around for a while. Into it you throw some good raw ingredients: a carrot, some onions, a potato or two. You leave it to simmer. Then you taste it. A little pepper, perhaps? It simmers a while longer. You taste it again. A sudden inspiration . . . lentils! You add lentils and a few beans for good measure. It's still a bit thin, not really tasty enough. You leave it to settle. The next day it tastes wonderful, more subtle, richer somehow. It's a good soup, perhaps even an exceptional soup and now it's ready to eat!

In my early days as a playwright I wanted to see writing a play as a completely logical process, akin to writing an essay or a factual article. I would make an intellectual decision concerning what I was going to write about; I would marshal my material, work out a schedule – a scene a day for example — then embark on my project. Is it any surprise that my early plays were often called 'schematic' since they were subject to a very rigid form of control? If I was unable to complete a piece of work I blamed characters who got out of hand or scenes which failed to evolve as planned. I was, in fact, at war with the natural process, trying hard to convince myself that there was nothing unpredictable or unmanageable about writing, that if I could organise myself sufficiently to get a university degree then I could surely write a play. It took a while to unlearn my education; indeed, I am still unlearning it. It has been a slow and painful experience.

My recent play, *Variations on a Theme by Clara Schumann,* provides a good example of the anarchic process at work. Someone gave me a copy of a biography of Clara Schumann with the words: "This would make a good subject for a play."

I read the book and found it interesting but I was by no means over-whelmed with enthusiasm. Much later the subject bobbed up in my mind, focussing this time on the particular aspect of Clara's life which had appealed to me more than any other: her relationship with the much younger Brahms. But I was still not sufficiently inspired to start writing.

However, for a variety of reasons, I convinced myself that I could repeat the process of my earlier play, *Self Portrait,* and write a large and basically biographical piece about the life of this undoubtedly remarkable woman, finding in it much relevance for the woman of today. So, what I was doing in effect was offering (albeit only to myself at first) a 'suitable' subject.

All through the lengthy period of research I experienced a strong feeling of resistance bordering on boredom. I was struggling to maintain an interest in this woman, having proclaimed her as my subject. But then, quite suddenly (and rather dramatically as it turned out during my research in Berlin), a very new perception of what I might be about to write broke through. What really interested me, I discovered, was something altogether less tangible than the facts of this woman's life. Why, for example, do we plunder the lives of others for subject matter? Is it in an attempt to understand our own a little better? Is Clara, after all, the subject of my play, or is the *real* subject the woman who thinks she will write about her? This released my imagination in a remarkable way. I had already written biography, now what I wanted to do was to write *about* it — to look at what makes up an individual, the different aspects of ourselves we need to acknowledge and incorporate in order to be whole. So the supposed subject was transformed. As it opened out it became immediately far more challenging, exciting and dangerous. I acknowledged that I was clinging on to the idea of pure biography as subject because, though moribund, it felt safer. Now I felt scared but revitalised. The idea had sprung to life. The soup, previously quite tasteless, had acquired a new, more pungent flavour.

That is not to say that you shouldn't write a play based on the life of a real person. But it could prove to be a stultifying rather than a liberating experience unless you can find an answer to the following questions.

Firstly: What is it in the subject's life that is of particular significance to you? Is there something which resonates strongly for you in that person's circumstances, attitudes or relationships?

Secondly: Can you find some reverberations in the events of the subject's life that will communicate strongly to an audience, enable them to empathise, to discover the similarities or appreciate the differences between that life and theirs? It won't be enough to recount events in a bland and uncritical way; you will need to make the material your own and communicate your involvement in it to your audience.

Don't be tempted to regard the biographical play as an easy option simply because it lets you off the hook of having to invent everything.

Existing documentation may provide you with an enormous amount of material but you will still need to sift and arrange this. It won't tell the story for you; you will still have to tell it yourself. The sheer weight of material may seem reassuring at first but can quickly become daunting. If you are dealing with the life of a great writer, or any other public figure, it's all too easy to be hypnotised by that person's reputation. You will then find it difficult to move away from what is the received wisdom to a response that is purely your own.

At the same time, whatever hooked you into the material — its particular significance for you — will have its painful as well as its pleasurable resonances for you as the work unravels.

Gill Brightmore, a workshop student, wanted to write about an imaginary meeting between Virginia Woolf and Sylvia Plath. She found many points of comparison between the two writers and felt that they had something to communicate which might be of relevance to their modern counterparts: women struggling to be writers.

She wrote to me early in the workshop: "I have made a shot at the Sylvia and Virginia play. As I began to get into it I found it quite 'painful', particularly assimilating the letters of Sylvia Plath. I've had to stop for a couple of days.

"With regard to the research itself, I've decided more or less to write the first draft and then work in any close references to the text in the second draft, and if I feel it is necessary to expand the theme. I thought I would never begin to write if I stopped to research items first.

". . . Stylistically, in the last section of the play, I have the idea of using two simultaneous monologues — of Sylvia and Virginia — and to some-how intercut them. I have also decided that the lives of the real Sylvia and Virginia, as well as the quotations from their work, should 'infiltrate' the text, as it were, and not stand out as 'set pieces'.

"I hope I can manage to do this, as well as begin writing again."

Gill continued to explore the possibilities of this through several drafts but did not, in the course of the workshop, feel that she had solved all the problems which the vast scope of the raw material had created. Later she said that she felt she had been too ambitious and would prefer to work on a more limited canvas in her next play. Yet I never regarded her work on this play as a failure or as time wasted. She had been extremely adventurous in her choice of subject and had, as an inevitable result, exposed herself to a great deal of danger. I think that the sheer size of what she was taking on had not occurred to her at first and she plunged in, regardless of her own safety. She in fact came very close to solving all the problems.

Pam Gems has sometimes chosen real people as the subjects for her plays.

Piaf tells the story of the street-wise urchin who became a world-famous singer. *Queen Christina* is based on the life of the Swedish queen who was brought up as a man in order to ensure succession to the throne. In *Queen Christina* Gems looks at the whole question of sex roles and moves towards a definition of femaleness which combines the qualities of strength and gentleness. *Piaf* too is very much about a search for female autonomy in a world in which power is usually vested in men.

Gems' choice of these women for her subject matter is quite deliberate in that she uses their biographies to illustrate her own viewpoint. Thus the subject matter does not act as a constraint but an opportunity. In *Piaf* in particular Gems is able to draw the attention of a very wide audience to issues which might not have inspired much interest if presented in a less entertaining form.

The only justification for writing a play based on the life of a real person is that there is something in that life which resonates very strongly for you and ignites in you a passionate commitment to communicate what you have felt.

The same is probably true of plays which have their origins in historic events, whether recent or distant. Obviously this is a very fruitful source of raw material for the writer, but only if the events are to be used by you, rather than you by them. I have read too many pedestrian dramatisations to think that the depiction of tragic, world-shattering or epoch-making incidents necessarily leads to the creation of a good play.

Such plays can excite and challenge the audience but only when the imagination has been sparked by a specific, possibly quite peripheral, aspect of an event and only where the writer's eye has been caught by a particular detail in the action.

Stephen Poliakoff, in his play *Breaking the Silence*, links the history of his own family and in particular the story of his grandfather with the events of a period of great upheaval in Russian history. The effects of those events on the lives of ordinary people are made to feel intensely personal. If we needed to know straight facts we could look in a history book; the play helps us to empathise with the real people who lived through the events.

Louise Page, in her fine play *Salonika*, looks at the First World War from an unfamiliar angle. She avoids the obvious already well-exposed aspects of war to explore more subtle themes. Her central character is a woman whose husband had died in the war, yet Page uses the events of the past to illuminate the present where men still die in futile combat and women are still left to pick up the pieces.

Both these plays, whilst based on events in the past, are in no sense 'historical' plays. They are about now or all time, about real people and not historical figures.

If you are interested in history as a potential source of subject matter you need to look beyond the headlines and the textbooks. It's not enough to read endless accounts of a particular event then to regurgitate them with a cast of a thousand or a cast of three. This may make a history lesson but it won't make a play.

If a particular event or period attracts you, once again you need to ask yourself 'why'? What is it that hooks into your obsession?

Sometimes writers are commissioned to write a play to celebrate or commemorate a particular event in a community; the same criteria still apply. You can't write about anything unless it excites you, unless you can find some aspect of it, however obscure, which will feed your particular imagination.

Some time ago I was asked to write a community play for the town of Ottery St Mary in Devon. I had never been there and knew nothing of its history. However, an enquiry at ground level presented me with an 'instant' subject — a fire in the 1860's, in which much of the town was destroyed. At first I wasn't especially interested in this topic: it meant nothing to me.

However, further investigation into old newspapers of the period revealed a particular incident following the fire: a brick chimney, long neglected and overdue for repair, had collapsed, killing several women and one child. All this had happened during an outdoor meeting at which a fiery young woman preached on a text from Revelations. I could feel a familiar sense of excitement, a sort of low level buzz in my creative sensors. The chimney should have been dismantled . . . who was to blame? Who were the women who had died and why were they there? The fire had destroyed many of the dwellings of the working people but the factory had mysteriously been saved . . . why? My imagination was beginning to take hold, causing me to select, subconsciously, those aspects of the raw material that had seemed, at first sight, so bland and unappealing. I was beginning to understand what I wanted and to look for what would feed my obsession. The 'objective' facts were rapidly becoming more and more subjective. And so the themes of the play, *The Ballad of Tilly Hake*, gradually came into focus.

I usually feel that I should sound a note of caution if a student says she intends to write a play about 'the unfair treatment of women in the work-place', 'materialism and greed in modern society', or 'our responsibility to the Third World'. This is not because these issues cannot constitute suitable or worthwhile material for a play (they patently can) but because I fear for the outcome when this is the starting point.

To return to Pat West's play about the builders . . . If she had begun with the statement . . . "I want to write a play about the position of women in patriarchy, about creativity and deconstruction, about the links between the ordinary worker and oppressed women in capitalist society", I might have felt far less optimistic than when she said: "Damn builders . . . noisy buggers with their transistor radios . . . climbing in and out of my windows . . . can't get on with my work . . . think I'll write a play about it!" (or words to that effect).

The first approach is basically non-dramatic and would be more suitable for an article or a letter to the newspapers. The second, focussing as it does on character and conflict, seems to pull naturally towards a play. It allows the writer to embody and explore the very same idea but in dramatic form.

Anne Challenor, a workshop student, felt she would like to write about how women respond to men's needs, subjugating their own, through fear of rejection. Her first draft, predictably, read like a piece of feminist polemic. Even though the politics were sound and powerfully expressed, the characters lacked individuality and the dialogue was rather stilted. We needed to dig for what lay behind this rather academic sounding subject to find the painful personal story in which this same dynamic was a salient factor. When encouraged to confront her real subject, Anne went on to explore feelings, rather than theories and to deal with real people rather than mouthpieces for ideas. The play, *Mirror Image*, improved beyond recognition.

I don't think there is a single issue that an audience cannot face as long as it is presented in a sufficiently dramatic form. But the ideas must be channelled through characters who have a vibrant life of their own and do not exist simply to serve the writer's preoccupations.

So, in *Road* by Jim Cartwright, the audience is subjected to a searing and highly political analysis of the impoverished quality of life of ordinary people in a beleaguered community. But Cartwright does not lecture us, he *shows* us. We see the young couple starving themselves to death in an empty room; we see the ugliness and futility of a drunken sexual encounter; we see the despair of people left to rot by the State. Till, finally, we witness, in an extraordinary and moving scene, the instinctive reaching out for something more, something beyond all the pain and suffering. The play strikes more effectively at our apathy and complacency than any political pamphlet because the characters are alive, speak for themselves and draw us powerfully into their deprived and painful world.

Similarly, in *Masterpieces* by Sarah Daniels, we have what is essentially a dramatic exploration of the theme of the relationship between pornography and violence against women, whilst Louise Page's *Tissue* looks at the issues surrounding women undergoing mastectomy and their interactions with the medical establishment.

Caryl Churchill, in *Cloud Nine*, looks at the issue of sexual stereotyping and the need to break free of repression. She proves that plays dealing with serious subjects do not necessarily have to be serious in form and explores her theme with an outrageous humour and a healthy disregard for any convention, theatrical or social.

The first half of the play is set in a Victorian colony, the second in contemporary (1979) London. Through a variety of bizarre and con-tradictory characters and scenes — Betty, for example, is played by a man, and Joshua, a black servant, is played by a white actor — Churchill breathes anarchic life into what might have seemed a highly academic subject. What is important is that the characters, however strange, do have autonomous life, a voice of their own. Churchill uses them to investigate and illustrate the debate she finds so interesting but she does not abuse them; they are people, not puppets.

One of the main aims of my 'Made in Wales' workshops was that they should provide an opportunity for women to explore their female experience and to draw on it as potential subject matter for their plays. This was to prove more difficult than it at first appeared. It was all too easy for the students to slip into an automatic response which created men as protagonists and women as passive bystanders.

However, there was an immense freedom to be found in discovering distinctive and appropriate ways of showing women's experience. I am not talking about polemic, agit-prop or soap-box drama, but about a dramatic expression of the female view, which gives a new validity both to the woman writer and to her audience. When 'allowed', in supportive surroundings, to explore these novel possibilities, the writers struggled towards finding and using, sometimes perhaps for the first time, their own authentic voice.

Many of the plays expressed a sense of this new-found liberty and the writers found they were able to deal with predominantly female preoccupations without fear or apology. Jane Buckler, in *Burd Mary,* writes about a young girl who is a charcoal-burner in the Forest of Dean. Using an historical context she deals movingly with abortion and the fiercely hostile reaction of society to a young woman who seeks her own autonomy.

Judy Leather's play, *Oysters and Onions,* looks at the strange dynamic between two women who grew up together in a children's home, with the anarchic character of an older woman, mother to one, adopted mother to the other, as a brooding and powerful presence throughout.

Helen Gwyn's play, *Echo Lady,* very different in concept, is a study of loneliness and alienation, concerning a group of misfits who meet to engage in a strange and private ritual. Using spells, rhyme and music, the play is tender, whimsical and poetic.

There is, of course, male and female in all of us, yin and yang, but we inhabit a world in which the masculine principle has predominated for too long. I believe that it's not only desirable but actually *essential* to redress that balance in whatever way we can.

In your search for subject matter, therefore, why not dare to look on the reverse side? Try to discover that aspect of the world, or your own nature, that has remained unexplored.

There are always stories to be told — stories about real but not famous people, which strike you as poignant or powerful and demanding to be heard. When I was a community worker on a bleak housing estate I met a woman who both moved and frightened me. She was the victim of long-term battering by a violent and often drunken husband and was fighting to bring up her children in extreme poverty. She frightened me because she was my age, but looked twice as old, because life had made her into a bully, because her personality — such an extraordinary mixture of self-destructiveness and sheer bloody-minded determination to survive — was a harsh reminder of the dual possibilities which exist in us all. Her story continued to haunt me long after I had left both the job and the area, and I felt absolutely impelled to communicate something of it to an audience. This became the basis of my play *Bed of Roses*, which portrayed a woman's struggle towards some sort of self-awareness and freedom.

Of course, it was pure fiction, and some might call it *romantic* fiction, since the woman in question had no autonomy. Poverty and illness looked set to destroy both her and the family she struggled to keep alive. So my play was in the nature of a dream built on a harsh reality — a hope for the future rather than a strict record of the present. Fiction based on fact.

Iris Long, a workshop student, had read a story in the papers about the suicide pact of an elderly couple. She was interested in what had prompted such a drastic decision and wanted to write about the ordinary people who had committed such an extraordinary act. Her play, *A Quiet Life,* tells the story she imagined behind the headlines. It is a fantasy but built on the possibilities offered by the short account of a real event.

People will always tell you stories. If they know you are a writer they will often say: "You ought to write about this!" But you will only hear what appeals to you; you will only be able to construct your imagined world on the basis of what ignites your particular passion or feeds into your particular preoccupation at the time. Iris was probably drawn to the snippet in the paper because she was asking herself the question: "Could I do that, given similar circumstances?"

There is no shortage of subject matter. You are literally surrounded by it, filled with it, if you can only train yourself to look, listen and be receptive to what goes on both within you and around you.

Failing all else, there are always dreams to stir your imagination. I dreamt the setting of my play *Bardo*. I saw a sun-bleached, abandoned hotel in a hot country. Outside, the distant sound of gunfire, at the window a torn white curtain. A telephone that doesn't work; a cracked mosaic floor. I don't know why I dreamt it but the image lodged itself in my brain and would not go away. Eventually I was forced to explore the hotel, to account for the gunfire, to create a story which could take place in the setting I had imagined in my dream.

Sometimes the genesis of a play is as mysterious and illogical as this. An image floats to the surface of the mind and demands recognition. A face spotted in a crowd insinuates itself into your consciousness, gradually acquiring a past, present and future. A snatch of conversation teases away in your brain until it starts to grow into a statement, a speech even, and from there becomes the focus for a scene which as yet has no reason to exist.

I think that I'm simply asking you to trust the process. Forget logic, try to unlearn most of what you've been taught. You are embarking on a rough journey without map or compass.

If you are speedy, over-organised or lack confidence in your own instincts, you will seize the first idea which comes into your head, hastily tie it down before it can run away, structure it, plan it and keep it under control. This may well result in a play but it will not be the most exciting play you could have written.

But, if you can just allow the alchemy to work, then the result may be chaotic or wonderful — or even a little of both. I am advocating lack of caution, an openness to all possibilities. This takes time: there is no instant and reliable formula. Sometimes the process works, sometimes it doesn't. Things may go underground and refuse to surface until they are ready to do so. This too is valuable and necessary.

Writing is, after all, a mysterious, even frightening process, and if you want to stop now before you get too embroiled, then perhaps this is as good a moment as any. It's rather like falling unsuitably in love. There's usually a moment when you could decide not to go on. Once that moment has passed, there's really no hope at all. You'll find yourself irrevocably hooked on all that excitement . . . all the pain, poetry and passion. There's no turning back then.

Sometimes the ideas come so thick and fast that you can't hold them all in your head at the same time. This is when your notebook might prove useful. Make a note of everything, whatever it is, or might be. You might like to date each entry in case you can later chart some kind of progress or see a pattern that might be emerging from the chaos. But try not to formalise anything at this stage. Fight against any preconceived notion of what the play will be about. Don't decide; don't prejudge; and, above all, don't panic.

The important thing is to be responsive, to keep the channels open. Your subject will gradually emerge out of the mass of undefined material, a shape will gradually define itself. If you look at the clouds for long enough you see sheep and dragons. If you gaze into the fire you see chrysanthemums and towers.

A collection of apparently unconnected thoughts, odd reactions to various events, people, stories; a merging of things overheard, glimpsed, remembered: these and many other stimuli will fuse into what you may identify, at last, as an 'idea'. At this point, and probably not before, you may feel ready to answer the question:

"What are you going to write about?"

Project: Activating your imagination

GO OUT WITH OPEN EARS AND EYES

Go to a busy place, such as a shopping precinct, railway station or sports centre. Observe what is going on and then:
  a) Make a note of any small incident which seemed intrinsically 'dramatic': a conflict, an example of pain, tension, etc.
  b) Describe the people involved and then invent names and life-histories for them.
  c) Speculate on how the incident might have developed and 'predict' a possible outcome.
Remember to reject the commonplace. Be as bizarre or outrageous as you like. The material is yours — the only truth is what you invent.

LOOK FOR A MEMORY OF A PARTICULAR EVENT IN YOUR LIFE

Locate a memory specifically in time and place and then:

    a) Describe what happened in as much detail as you can.
    b) Describe how you felt at the time.
    c) Describe how you feel about it now.
    d) Explain what it is about this memory that still resonates for you.
    e) Analyse why you selected this particular memory rather than another.
    f) Ask yourself why this memory should be of interest to anyone else.

LISTEN TO ELDERLY PEOPLE TALKING ABOUT THEIR LIVES

Ask an elderly person to tell you about her/his life. Listen carefully to what she/he has to say and then consider the following:

    a) Has the person had a happy life?
    b) Have there been any regrets, triumphs, hopes, fears?
    c) Can you pinpoint a single event which seems especially potent – a turning point, perhaps?
    d) Could you rewrite the biography so as to give the events a different outcome?

CHAPTER THREE

Research

– Locating the facts – Delving into the subject –
– Observation – Keeping a notebook –
– Using documentary material – Setting up a filing system –
– Reference books – Historical and period research –
– The personal interview – Speech and dialects –
– The selection process –
– **Project: Testing the boundaries** –

A simple definition of 'research' is whatever you feel you need to know before you are ready to start writing.

What you research, and how, will depend very much on personal preference and temperament: nobody can really tell you exactly how to go about it. It's both a creative and a selective process which many writers admit to finding more enjoyable than the act of writing itself.

In one way research is nothing special at all, since it is what you are already doing every moment of your life: looking, listening, exploring new sensations, meeting new people, finding out how things work, travelling to new places either in fact or in your imagination, absorbing the significance of world events or personal experiences, reading, watching films or television, mentally filing away a mass of constantly evolving information and attempting to impose some order on it. All this is in the nature of research, even if it's not directed towards any specific piece of work.

It will certainly be an advantage if you can retain an almost childlike sense of enquiry. It will prevent your research from turning into an academic exercise, transforming it instead into an incredible journey, which will both enrich and inform the play you are about to write.

A writer's research falls into two broad categories. The first is simply a question of locating or verifying the facts you need for the further development of your idea. You are looking for some specific, already

45

identified information: dates, figures, details concerning an historical period. You may already know where to look for this information or, when you discover where it is to be found, you will easily be able to locate it and utilise it.

The second category involves a much more fluid process. You know you want to find out something but you don't yet know what it is. You will need to identify some possible areas of exploration, then you will embark on your journey. You have no real idea as yet of your ultimate destination, nor of what you will encounter on the way. You hope that your discoveries will help you to write the play you already have in mind but it is impossible, at this stage, to be certain.

Sometimes what you take to be the first process transforms itself imperceptibly into the second, as you are drawn down fascinating and uncharted by-ways by each fresh discovery. Perhaps the word 'research' conjures up an image of a dusty library, long, tedious hours spent making copious notes while the sun shines just outside the window. Imagine instead a perfumed garden, overgrown with rare and beautiful plants, or a forest of intertwined branches and shady paths which draw the traveller off-course with their seductive promise of undiscovered delights.

Writing a play is a quest, a journey through space and time, and your period of research is your first encounter with all the pleasures and perils that lie ahead.

Of course, there are some plays which require no research at all, since the material is already present in your imagination or your memory. But, for the purpose of this chapter, let's assume that there are some things, or even many things, which you will need to look into before you can begin.

First of all, there's no need to panic. Don't be tempted to jettison the subject which has taken so long to surface just because you are conscious of vast gaps in your knowledge. If you regard it as a challenge rather than a disadvantage, there's much enjoyment to be found in tracking down the information you need. Finding out things is not difficult, if you know how to go about it, where to look and whom to ask. You don't need an academic background or any particular qualifications: all you need is an enquiring mind, a certain amount of patience and a sense of adventure.

I think that I have often deliberately set myself problems in the subject matter of my plays for the sheer challenge of trying to find solutions. I have never liked things to be too easy. Indeed, I'm sure that one of my subconscious criteria when deciding upon the subject of a new play is that I should be able to discover something new in the process of writing it.

I positively relish the thought of uncovering some aspect of the world previously unknown to me; far from deterring me from exploring a particular subject, I find that my lack of specialist knowledge actually acts as a stimulus and an incentive.

These Animals Are Dangerous, which I wrote for radio, is set in a zoo, where Flack, the Keeper of the Ape House, locks himself up in a cage with a gorilla as a protest against many things, including the Management. I think that the idea first took root when I saw a keeper at Bristol Zoo sitting quietly in a family group of gorillas, all of them surveying the human onlookers with a mixture of amusement and sadness. On another occasion I was sure that I saw a gorilla meditating, which made me wonder whether these animals might have something of special value to communicate to us.

To say that I knew nothing about gorillas would be an understatement, but by then I was too excited by the idea to let this stand in my way. I mapped out a plan of action.

The research I undertook involved a study of literature, factual information and film. I also spent many hours talking to the Zoo-Keeper and to other officials at the zoo. I took numerous photographs and made several tapes of both men and animals.

But most of all I watched gorillas — eating, sleeping, playing or just sitting, and I watched people watching them. I learnt a great deal about the animals and perhaps more than I'd bargained for about zoos and the people who run them.

I was always conscious that, in the time available, I could only form impressions rather than actually amass any expertise on the subject. But since I was hoping to write a play rather than a thesis on gorilla behaviour what little I discovered proved sufficient to give me some confidence in portraying both the animal and the situation with some authenticity.

I think that it's important to get your facts right. Firstly, because if you don't, then the whole basis of your work falls into question. If the audience can't trust you to give an accurate picture of what can easily be verified, then how can they trust you to create believable characters or situations?

Secondly, it will give you confidence if you feel that you know what you are talking about. Your research will inevitably cover a far wider range of topics than you will ever need for your play but this background will add texture and subtlety to your work. Work that is poorly or inadequately researched invariably feels thin and threadbare. The aim is not to parade your new-found knowledge but to incorporate it, to react to it, to learn from it, then to make it invisible.

The first step in your research plan is to survey what you already have at your fingertips and decide how much additional material you will need to feel confident.

Once you have decided where the main gaps in your knowledge lie it might be useful to make a list of what you need to find out and possible sources of this information. You might also make a note of questions you need to ask, of places which might be worth a visit, of people who might be able to help, of books which might contain useful information. This list can be as much of a jumble as you like; just try to make it as comprehensive as you can at this stage. You need to be able to assess the size of the problem. Organisation and method can follow later.

The first few pages of my notebook for my play *Self Portrait* read as follows:

1.   Germaine Greer: *The Obstacle Race* (order)
2.   Courtauld Institute re Twitchin (Portman Square behind Selfridges). *Gwen John: Her Art and Her Religion* M.A. Report, May 1972
3.   Michael Holroyd (not free March)
4.   British Museum Newspaper Library
5.   National Museum of Wales: Cardiff
6.   Victoria Hotel, Tenby
7.   Oxford: Ashmolean
8.   David Fraser Jenkins: Tate
     London: Tate Archives (Thurs. or Frid)
                      National Art Museum (V + A)
                      Ben John?
9.   Aberystwyth: National Library of Wales

Write to Le Havre
Questions
1.   Vera Oumançoff. Who found letters etc? Where are they now?
2.   Who took G.J. to hospice? How did they identify her?
3.   Where is she buried?
4.   Living relatives?
Romilly John: wrote 8.2.86
Letters: Musée Rodin, Paris

Research can take as much or as little time as you decide to allow yourself. In the case of *Self Portrait* it was to involve me in a great deal of travelling, to London, Oxford, the New Forest, Manchester, Cardiff, Aberystwyth and, finally, Paris. I read literally thousands of letters and notes in manuscript form, visited many galleries and museums, interviewed experts and others. In all it was a process which lasted about six months and could have gone on much longer had I not been writing to a specific deadline.

Research clearly costs money as well as time. In this particular case I was fortunate enough to be working under commission from Theatr Clwyd who generously paid for me to travel to Paris in the company of a translator whose French was a great deal better than mine. This enabled me to read the letters Gwen wrote to her lover, Auguste Rodin, and his (occasional) replies in their original French.

If this is your first play, or even your second, you will probably not have the luxury of either a commission fee or expenses to cover the cost of travel. This is where you will need to weigh things in the balance. Is it worth speculating the cost of a few train fares to gain specific information not available to you closer to home? If you feel that the answer is 'no', then you may need to limit your research to what can realistically be achieved without incurring too much expense. This may be frustrating but it is also, unfortunately, one of the facts of life of being a writer. You will often feel that practical considerations such as time and money inhibit the free flow of your creativity. You will learn to become ingenious at devising viable (and cheaper) alternatives to the plan you first thought of. You will become amazingly resilient at bouncing back when your most exciting schemes fail or are impeded by practical considerations.

As far as equipment is concerned there's really no need to involve yourself in any great expense. A small tape-recorder might be useful if you intend to interview people, though taping is not always either possible or desirable. If you decide to buy some books rather than borrow them from libraries a highlighter will help you to identify important passages for future reference. When you are working with original manuscripts, of course, you must always take care not to mark them in any way.

Since I have already proclaimed myself a total Luddite when it comes to the miracles of modern technology, I can hardly now sing the praises of the 'on-line' computer which will call up material on any given subject at the touch of a button. I know that other writers find electronic data-bases amazingly useful but it will certainly be no impediment to you in your research if you have nothing more elaborate than a pencil, a notebook and a desire to find out.

It is helpful, however, to devise some simple method of codifying and retaining the information you gather as your research progresses. If you don't do this you will only waste time and create confusion for yourself. Again, there's no need for any elaborate system. A ring file with dividers is useful so that you can classify information alphabetically or under subject headings and a card-index with separate categories for books, people, places, etc., will help you to keep track of the information you collect. Never forget that the research is only a means to an end, not an end in itself. If you find yourself buying a mountain of matching folders and brightly coloured highlighters just remind yourself that none of these can actually write the play for you. But don't be too strict with yourself. If a handsome red notebook makes you feel confident every time you pick it up, then it is doing a good job. If you need the 'tools of the trade' to convince yourself that you are really a writer, then so be it. As long as you realise that there will come a time to lay aside the ring files, the tape recorders, the card indexes and all the paraphernalia, and simply get on with the task of writing.

In the meanwhile, you are 'engaged in research'. Where can you find what you are looking for?

Published texts are an obvious and easily accessible source of information. Remember, however, that all writers are biased; you should never rely on any one book as an authority, but should try to read around your subject as much and as widely as time will allow, in order to form as rounded a picture as possible. Whether or not you take copious notes as you read is a matter of personal preference. There is, however, no point in taking any notes at all, unless you propose to review them and extrapolate from them afterwards. Too many notes may simply prove daunting and indigestible.

Every writer has her favourite reference books. I find the *Encyclopaedia Brittanica* very helpful in opening up the whole field of enquiry on any subject and pointing the way to further research. *Whitaker's Almanack* and the *Statesman's Year Book* both provide quick access to information on any given year.

Ann Hoffmann's excellent book *Research for Writers* offers an exceptionally comprehensive guide to where to look for material, as well as making some sensible suggestions about research methodology. The book is worth buying for its first appendix alone, which gives a selective list of major sources in the United Kingdom. There are also lists of books which might prove useful in historical and factual research, as well as detailed information on libraries and archives.

Sometimes, particularly if you are researching into the life of a real person, it can be valuable to look at original, unpublished material such as letters, notebooks and diaries. Simply handling a letter written by your subject can be a strangely moving experience, and hours spent poring over indecipherable and often inconsequential notes can give you an extraordinary sense of being 'in contact', which no printed book can ever evoke.

Most libraries with archives of original manuscripts require you to obtain a reader's ticket before you can gain access to the material. This is for obvious reasons of security, since the papers are, of course, unique. The reader's ticket is only a formality and need not present an obstacle. You go to the library in question and fill in a simple form. You are sometimes required to give a reference. It's best to allow yourself plenty of time for this as there's nothing more frustrating than arriving with exactly one hour to spare, and fifty letters to read, only to be barred at the door by an official demanding references.

If you are going to make a special journey to look at original material it's probably better to write in advance to arrange your visit and to ensure that the material in question is actually available to you and not temporarily in America or Australia. Archivists are natural enthusiasts for the material in their care so they are usually incredibly helpful and rather pleased that you actually want to look at what they have spent years sorting out.

Ceridwen Lloyd-Morgan at the National Library of Wales became my friend and ally during my research on Gwen John. I found her an invaluable source of information as well as a great support. She undoubtedly made my life a good deal easier by pointing me in the direction of relevant material and helping me to avoid some of the more obvious pitfalls.

Looking at letters and diaries can be both fascinating and infuriating. Perhaps, as I found when researching the life of Clara Schumann, the handwriting is practically indecipherable or the material in a foreign language. Perhaps there is just so much material that it threatens to overwhelm you as you sift through endless trivia looking for the one item which will prove significant.

But, whatever the problems, as you prise open the first box, you will feel that you have discovered a treasure trove, a cache of secret delights.

There is always another, more disturbing aspect to reading personal papers: a sense of being an unlicensed eavesdropper, of prying into matters which are essentially very private and were never intended for public scrutiny. Looking at such material always makes me wonder uncomfortably which of my own very personal letters may one day fall into the hands of strangers. Certainly, as I sat in the Musée Rodin in Paris, watching the snow fall on Rodin's 'Thinker' outside, and reading the thousands of pathetic little notes which Gwen John sent to her famous lover, I was filled with a strange mixture of pity and fury, tinged with a sense of guilt that time had allowed me access to these very personal documents.

The Public Record Office in Kew is a favourite haunt of many a writer, and houses a fund of fascinating material giving a detailed insight into life in a particular area in the past. Records go back to the 11th Century. Parish registers, marriage indexes, school record books, registers of births and deaths — all these can provide you with specific data in answer to already formulated questions. Alternatively they can simply stimulate your imagination and offer a whole range of possibilities for you to build on.

Similarly graveyards . . . . As I was slowly drawn towards the subject of *The Ballad of Tilly Hake*, my Ottery St Mary community play, I began to haunt the local graveyard, looking for verification of the theories I was already formulating. Seeing the name in print of one of your intended characters is endorsing enough; seeing it engraved on a tombstone is awe-inspiring. I knew that I was going to write about real people, people who had lived and worked in the town in Victorian times, but seeing the actual grave was a very important moment for me.

It's quite difficult to convey how this works in practice since it is far from being a logical process. Something you read, see or hear suddenly clicks and sets off a new and important train of thought, or causes already present ideas to re-form in some new configuration. This can often be an important turning point in your research, the moment at which you feel the play spring to life, like a baby quickening in the womb.

If you are still in pursuit of information, you will find old and current newspapers an excellent source of material.

The British Museum Newspaper Library at Colindale (opposite the Underground Station) has back copies of newspapers and periodicals available to readers. You will need a reader's ticket but a short-term ticket is available on application. If you know exactly what you want to look at photocopies may be ordered by post.

When looking at old newspapers don't expect to be able to restrict yourself to reading specific items; your eye will inevitably be irrestistibly drawn by news reports, fashion items and advertisements which have nothing whatsoever to do with your research. Of course, they *are* relevant (though you may not yet have realised it), and you should allow yourself enough time to enjoy browsing. Whilst researching my play *Geraniums*, which deals with events which took place in East London in the 1930's, I spent many absorbing hours reading back copies of *The Daily Worker* (before it became *The Morning Star*) at the newspaper's offices in London. Contemporary accounts of the event in which I was interested — the Battle of Cable Street — were far more revealing than the descriptions in books written after the event. It was particularly useful to read the various opinions regarding the appropriate course of action to be taken, rather than the retrospective analyses offered by history books.

Similarly, the blatantly anti-Semitic diatribes of Mosley and his followers in the Fascist newspapers of the 1930's cast an ugly light on his subsequent disclaimers in the press.

Newspapers give a highly selective account of events and as such they are an invaluable way to gauge the extremes of public opinion as expressed by the media at a particular point in history. But it's essential to read more than one account, since they are always written with extreme bias. *The Times* and *The Morning Star*, taken in conjunction, will give a far more balanced picture than one or the other.

My understanding of the events which took place in October 1936 was also greatly enhanced by watching contemporary newsreel. Books could tell me that the police only exercised necessary restraint in dealing with the mass of Jewish protesters and their sympathisers, who gathered to prevent Mosley and his followers from marching through the East End streets. The newsreel enabled me to see with my own eyes that this was not exactly the truth, whilst the commentary gave me unequivocal evidence of the bias of the media against the 'protesters'.

If you are concerned about historical accuracy and like to be able to build up a detailed visual picture for yourself, then museums specialising in equipment and costume may prove helpful. Local-interest museums are to be found in many rural areas and these usually house an impressive collection of artifacts from the region.

All this will help you to visualise your characters in more specific detail, to imagine them at work or at leisure, to get inside their skins and feel what it is to *be* them. You will know what kind of clothes they wore, the tools they used, the conditions they lived in. These things may seem quite obvious but it is surprising how many writers fail to capture the flavour of a specific historical period. Again, it's not a question of overloading your play with historical detail just for its own sake, but of absorbing sufficient information to feel comfortable and familiar in the world you are creating.

Sometimes similar research is necessary for a contemporary play which inhabits a world that is unfamiliar to you. For example, for a play set in a hospital you will need to have some understanding of hospital routine and hierarchy, of equipment and current practices. All this information can be much more easily obtained on the spot than from a book. Your eyes and ears are your best allies: what you see and hear for yourself will invariably prove far more interesting and rather less anodyne than what anyone else will tell you. Don't be afraid of your lack of expertise. Sometimes the inexpert eye intuitively sees more clearly, cutting through layers of carefully arranged obfuscation of the truth.

Don't forget that you are in the process of creating your own world, not simply reporting back on the world which exists. Therefore, if something *seems* to be so to you, then so be it, no matter what the official view.

If you need information about a particular profession or trade, there is no better way to glean it than by spending time with someone who practises it, watching, listening and trying to understand what goes on beneath the surface.

You usually learn more from what people *don't* tell you, or even from what they wilfully distort or hide, than from what they willingly discuss in great detail. Try not to be either too naive or too analytical. Naivety will lead you to believe everything you are told without question, to accept everything at face value. If you are over-analytical you will not allow for the many layers of reality which make up any situation. You can't expect something of great complexity to yield itself up to you at the first encounter. You may already have formed a viewpoint about the subject of your research and be looking for evidence to support it. Nevertheless, you will learn more if you keep your mouth shut and let your informants speak or go about their business without too much active intervention on your part. Your role is simply to be open to everything, waiting, listening, learning.

Just a few days spent in a geriatric day hospital gave me a fairly clear picture of the problems of the staff who work there. I observed the huge gap between the ideal and the reality in patient care; the actual day to day routines; the crucial political issues, such as under-funding and under-staffing; the range of opinion from reactionary to radical. It is surprising how quickly you can absorb the feel of a place if you are receptive and curious.

People are usually eager to talk to an outsider and often hopeful that what you write will draw attention to their particular opinion. This does, of course, raise certain ethical questions. People will talk to you quite freely and in good faith. Sometimes, in a rush to communicate, they damn themselves out of their own mouths. Often they have clear and definite expectations of how they would wish you to make use of the information they are so readily giving. They will, quite naturally, be extremely disappointed, or possibly even enraged, when you present their stories from a different angle.

It seems important to be clear on two counts. Firstly, you should never lie about your motives. You are gathering background material for a play. Since you may not at this early stage actually know how this will feature in your finished work, it's probably better to err on the side of vagueness rather than give hard and fast assurances that will later be broken.

Secondly, it is as well to remember that the information you are being given is simply the opinion of the person telling you. It may be subject to strange emphasis, exaggeration or omission. It may even be a mass of deliberate lies. You may receive it in good faith but you must interpret it as you see fit. Whilst you will have no intention of distorting the facts, you cannot allow yourself to be inhibited or limited by the sensibilities of other people. You must present the truth as you see it.

It's obviously best to avoid causing offence or pain to those who are giving up their time in an attempt to help you. For this reason I usually try to explain that a play is a work of the imagination; that the factual information they will give me may appear in any form in the finished product; that they can in no way be held responsible for it. I offer them no assurances as to how their revelations will be used, and if they seek such assurances, I admit that I can't give them. This gives them the choice of participating or not.

People invariably ask one question: "Will I end up in your play?" The answer is: "If you do, you probably won't recognise yourself."

Sometimes it's very helpful to conduct a formal in-depth interview, particularly to obtain eye-witness accounts of a particular event. But this is where you will need to be very sensitive and responsive. Roger Stennett interviewed former Battle of Britain pilots for his play *Out of the Sun*. The events they recalled had often been traumatic, involving personal injury or the death of colleagues. These were the actual people you read about in the history books. The stories they had to tell were not at all objective: they were based on personal memories that were still painful. Such interviews demand great tact and skill and can take many patient hours. It is insensitive to attempt to interview an elderly man at speed, since he will undoubtedly regard your visit as a great event, an unusual opportunity to discuss past glories or recall poignant moments. Out will come the photographs, the diaries and all the memorabilia. There will probably be a splendid tea laid on in your honour. It may be your play, but it is his life.

Whatever the final outcome, you are bound to feel some sense of responsibility or privilege at being allowed to share in these important memories. Similar sensitivity is required when you interview the surviving relatives of famous figures who may form the subject of a play. What may seem entertaining or funny on the page may, in real life, have been humiliating or embarrassing. Someone who appears to you as amusingly eccentric or bizarrely interesting may have had a less positive effect on relatives or friends. Don't forget that the tragic events you are hoping to make the pivot of your drama involved real people with real emotions and vulnerabilities.

Never assume that people will automatically enjoy being interviewed or that they will agree to your using a tape-recorder for the purpose.

Many people find the presence of a tape inhibiting or even frightening. Some don't even like you to take notes. People like to talk but if what comes out proves unexpectedly distressing you may find yourself involved in a little amateur counselling.

If you are hoping to write in a particular dialect or to depict a character who speaks in an accent which is unfamiliar to you, then you will need to listen to people or tapes before you begin to write. It's not difficult to tune your ear to a strange dialect — it's a little like learning a foreign language. Your ear gradually adjusts till you begin to distinguish right and wrong usage. I always find it useful to 'hear' a character's voice in my head. Sometimes I will model a character's voice on that of a person I've met or heard who speaks in a way I think would be appropriate. Listening to ordinary people talking in the street, in buses, on trains is essential research for a writer and should become second nature to you, even when you have no particular project in mind.

The important thing is not to let gaps in your knowledge present an insurmountable problem. There is no need to jettison a subject simply because it involves matters which are unfamiliar to you. If you know where to look, it's usually possible to find out whatever you need to know.

However, there are genuine problems connected with research, some of which I have already touched upon. A major obstacle is obviously lack of time or money. If you find that you can't spare the time to research the project you have in mind, or if your research plan will involve you in more travel than you can afford, then you may be forced to have a radical rethink. This may not turn out to be a disadvantage at all; in fact it can help to focus the mind. If you know that you can't travel to France or Spain or wherever, then you may have to make a different kind of internal journey to find the material you need.

It's quite possible to do too much research and to find yourself totally submerged under a mass of material. This can have one of two results, both of them rather counter-productive.

One outcome is that you become totally obsessed with the research itself. You can't be parted from it; you are seduced down every by-way, every tortuous path leading nowhere. On the way you quite forget what you were supposed to be doing there in the first place. Several months later, you are the author of a great many scribbled notes but, alas, no play.

Another possible outcome is that you become strangely mesmerised by all that you read and are told. You develop such respect for the written word or for the statements of your interviewees that you dare not impose any imaginative gloss onto the material. "It must be true, because they say it is", becomes your motto. The result is that you may become an authority on your subject but you won't write a play.

Conflicting authorities can also cause writer's paralysis. You may read or listen to so many accounts of an event you simply can't see the wood for the trees, nor can you find anything you would dare to call the truth amongst all the evidence.

Copyright material may also prove problematical. Can you use it in your play? Will you need permission, and if so, from whom? The law of copyright is complex but don't be deterred if the material is really vital to you. Read the section in the *Writers' and Artists' Yearbook* for advice. Ann Hoffmann's *Research for Writers* is also useful on this subject.

The main thing to remember is that a play is a work of the imagination. It is not an academic essay or a piece of journalism. Your aim is to create your own world and to people it with characters that your audience will believe in and emphathise with. Whether you are writing about people who really existed, or people who never existed till you created them, your play is its own reality. It will be a world you have made in your own image.

The purpose of research is to supply you with evidence for your biased viewpoint, to support the ideas you have already begun to formulate. There is nothing objective in this process. You must make the facts work for you in the way which best suits your creative purpose.

Since research should always be viewed as a means to an end, you have to know when to stop. When I visited the biographer Michael Holroyd in the course of my research on Gwen John, he said: "You have to draw the line somewhere." There is always new material which could be looked at; there is always one more book you could read, one more person you could interview. Sooner or later you will have taken from it all it can teach you; you will have absorbed the essence of all you have heard, seen and been told, and must begin to make the material your own.

Yet research is definitely part of the creative process: your first step into unknown territory. It can sometimes be a surprisingly intense experience as you begin to engage more and more intimately with your subject.

I visited Meudon, the hilly suburb of Paris where Gwen John spent the last years of her life living as a virtual recluse in a small wooden shack in the rue Babie. The day I arrived there with Jan, my translator, it had been snowing. The house in whose garden the little hut stood was up for auction on the very next day. I climbed the wall to peep over. At that moment a young man with a polaroid camera (an estate agent? a spy from the art world?) clambered over and took a picture of the shack. He offered it to me without knowing why I wanted it.

The next day the place called to me so strongly that I had to return alone. I walked the distance between rue Babie and the substantial and respectable house which had been the home of Vera Oumançoff, for whom Gwen had developed a characteristically 'unsuitable' passion in later life. Afterwards I went on to Rodin's studio and found the bushes where Gwen had lain in wait, hoping to catch a glimpse of her 'Master'. I learnt, that is to say experienced, more about Gwen John in those few days than in weeks of reading books about art. For a few hours I felt almost too identified with my subject. I felt that I knew just what it had been like to live in that shack, to look out at the poplar trees, to walk to the austere Catholic Church, to stand outside the affluent house of her friend whom she was allowed to visit for just one hour every Monday, and to trudge up the almost perpendicular hill to the home of her renowned but never-present lover, Rodin.

I confronted the *real* subject of my play during that visit, realising that my interest in Gwen John was far from academic. I found myself appalled and fascinated by her loneliness and self-imposed isolation, knowing my own propensity towards reclusiveness. I was interested in the constant conflict she experienced between work and passion, and in the dichotomy between the mature and productive artist and the almost childlike woman who forgot to eat and slept with her feet in the open air so that she would wake in time for Mass. There could be no other title for the play but *Self Portrait*.

Variations on a Theme by Clara Schumann took me on another kind of personal journey . . .

Since I was to write about a pianist and composer I decided that I needed to do some 'action research' and embarked, as a totally unmusical adult, on the daunting task of learning to play the piano. My initial intention was simply to get a rough idea of the rudiments of playing and to learn to read music. (In fact I became completely engrossed in the piano and am still playing.)

My research took me to Berlin, both East and West, via a number of libraries, concerts, museums and archives. My ostensible purpose was to look at some archive material and Schumann memorabilia in a museum in East Germany. What actually happened on that often painful journey is that I gradually came to terms with my deep reservations about the play I thought I was going to write, and discovered another, quite different, play. Even so, no journey is ever totally abortive and no research process completely wasted. I needed to spend time looking at the material in order to discover that it was recalcitrant and impenetrable. I needed to understand what had persuaded me to attempt to come to terms with it in the first place. My real research was not, as it transpired, into the life of Clara Schumann, but into my own motivation. The play I went on to write, although it had its roots in the material I had been researching, was very different from the play I had originally planned.

Project: Testing the boundaries

MAKE A LIST

▷ Decide on a subject and make a list of what you feel you need to know before you start writing.
▷ Try to discover where you can find these things out.
▷ Divide the list into:
    a) Information to be found in books.
    b) People you might interview.
    c) Places you might visit.
▷ Make a list of questions which demand an answer.

DO SOMETHING YOU'VE NEVER DONE BEFORE

▷ Visit an amusement arcade/betting shop/skating rink/grand hotel.
▷ Sit up all night on Paddington Station.
▷ Learn to parachute/sky-dive/hang-glide/wind-surf.
▷ Gain first-hand experience of something which frightens or excites you and then:
    a) Note down your reactions and the reactions of others to you.
    b) Make a note of anything particularly bizarre, thought-provoking, painful or funny.
    c) Make a note of anything which stimulated your curiosity, made you angry or made you laugh.

CHAPTER FOUR

Characters and Dialogue

— Creating a character from observation —
— Writing a life history — Developing the personality —
— Motivation — External and internal conflict —
— Avoiding the stereotype — The historical character —
— Identifying the protagonist — Why *these* people? —
— Choosing names — Assigning status and roles —
— The first entrance — Writing believable dialogue —
— Telling lies — The power of silence — The 'through line' —
— How many characters? — Potential for change —
— **Project: Creating a character** —

The American playwright David Mamet wrote: "The dramatist's job is to create drama which proceeds from character and culminates in a surprising and inevitable conclusion."

Creating believable characters, and giving each an authentic and distinctive voice, is perhaps the most important aspect of writing a play. Until you have discovered and established your characters your play must remain an idea in your head or on the page. Only through them can it achieve three-dimensional reality.

The characters you invent will be brought to life by actors, whose main source of information is what you tell them in your text. It is their job to interpret your intentions as clearly as possible to the audience.

At the first read-through of a play an actor will often question the writer about a character's motivation, habits, education, his life outside the action of the actual play, his taste in clothes, food, preferred choice of holiday, etc. This is because the actor needs very specific information in order to portray the person you have imagined. The actor can't see inside your head so the information needs to be there on the page and it needs to be particular, detailed, consistent and, above all, credible. That's why it's so essential for you to know your characters intimately and to depict them strongly so that they can walk off the page with conviction. Thin or underdeveloped characterisation will undermine the authenticity of your play more profoundly than any other fault in the writing.

The process of devising characters is based on a mixture of observation, intuition and quite calculated decision-making.

Imagine yourself for a moment in, let's say, a doctor's waiting room. A woman enters. Even as she opens the door you can immediately observe a great deal about her from her external appearance. Her clothes, her walk, her posture, her facial expression, her obvious mannerisms, the way in which she regards the other occupants of the room — all these factors contribute to your first impression of who she is, what she wants, what she might do. Then she comes to sit next to you and begins a conversation. Now you are able to glean much more information. Accent, syntax, vocabulary, mode of delivery, as well as the actual content of what is said, all contribute clues. You quickly begin to build up a mental picture of who she is, or perhaps who she would like you to think she is: her motivation, her present state of mind, any particular circumstances she either reveals or tries to conceal. You may also gain some sense of her lifestyle, her aspirations, her fears, her hopes.

Perhaps you report back on what you have observed to a third party: "I met this woman at the doctor's. She was very smartly dressed . . . she looked like the wife of a successful businessman, or perhaps a dentist or a lawyer. She was really nervous . . . she kept twisting and twisting her wedding ring. She'd made her finger quite raw. I noticed that she'd been crying. She said her husband was away on business, but I reckon he'd just left her . . ."

One method of developing a character is, in effect, to reverse this almost automatic everyday process of registering, absorbing and deducing. Let's say that you are intending to write a play about a woman whose husband has just left her. You visualise her as well-dressed, well-groomed. You know that she is determined to keep up appearances. But today she has put on a little too much make-up in an attempt to hide the fact that she has been crying. She keeps twisting her wedding ring. All this is the product of your imagination, probably drawing on various different sources. Of course, it's only a starting point. Before she can come to life you will need to find out more about her, imagining what she is like outside the action of the play as well as within it. She will need a childhood, a set of memories, an environment, interests, obsessions, friends, relatives. None of these may figure in any way in the play you are to write but they are the fabric out of which your character is to be woven.

Or you could begin in a different way. Perhaps you have met an *actual* woman who interests you. Her external appearance, manner, walk, speech rhythms, and so on will not have to be imagined since you have already observed them in real life. But, unless she is very well-known to you, you may need to invent a history, a biography, fears, hopes and desires, to blend with what you have already observed.

I often ask students to do this as an exercise in creating a character. First, they must look for a real person whose external appearance interests them, or stimulates their imagination. I ask them to absorb as much detail as they can, to pick up as many clues as possible from dress, walk, skin, hair, mannerisms. Then I ask them to put words into their character's mouth, letting her speak at length either to herself or to someone who, for the purposes of this exercise, doesn't interrupt. This monologue, which should reveal what is uppermost in her mind, what currently obsesses or distresses her, brings her to life in another dimension.

A person's external appearance and manner answers the question: "Who do I want you to think I am?" It says: "This is the self I choose to project to the outside world."

Of course, in the case of mental disorder or insanity, severe and incapacitating illness, extremes of age or youth, or indeed any situation where an individual has little control or choice regarding how others will perceive her, the picture presented to the world is random, unmonitored and therefore uncensored. But in most other circumstances people make specific choices about how they present themselves to others.

On Monday, for example, I may decide to play the colourful extrovert. I dress in bright colours, wear dramatic earrings. I tell funny stories, making people laugh at my bizarre and unconventional behaviour. On Tuesday I may appear as the introverted academic, dressed in drab clothes, speaking quietly and in controlled tones, choosing every word with care.

There will be other aspects of my external appearance which are less completely under my control. They will indicate my state of health, hint at my state of mind, reveal my age, race, economic status, nationality, all of which will be more or less apparent, depending on the extent to which I am prepared to reveal or conceal them.

Now we penetrate to the second layer. The question now is: "Who do *I* think I am?" ie what are my private fears, hopes, desires, obsessions? These are the aspects of personality usually kept hidden from the world, and probably not at all evident in the self or selves we normally present in public. Nevertheless, these factors will contribute significantly to our actions.

There is a still deeper layer to penetrate. "Who am I really?" is the question. What is there in my make-up that I can't, as yet, acknowledge, even to myself. Is there something in my personal history or psychology which subconsciously motivates me, which colours my life and relation-ships? What really makes me tick?

If you think of your characters as existing on all these levels you will see that you need to know them as well or perhaps even better than you know your closest friend. Only then can they spring to life with all the ambiguity, richness and subtlety of real human beings rather than the simplistic one-dimensional crudity of cardboard cut-outs.

And yet, as with all creative processes, the development of characters is not an entirely logical procedure. Sometimes it feels less as if you are creating a character than that she is creating herself, evolving at her own pace, and with a will of her own, over which you have little control. The novelist Alice Walker experienced this phenomenon during the writing of her novel *The Colour Purple.* She describes the sensation of entering a room and finding her characters already there, sitting and talking, as it were, behind her back. It was an experience she found both energising and, at times, deeply disorientating.

There is no doubt that characters have this disturbing tendency to develop a mind of their own, wriggling out of your grasp into joyously anarchic independent life. Sometimes it seems as if you only gradually get to know them. You simply start the engine, then they grab the steering wheel out of your hands and drive you off on some unknown and unplanned route.

I often hear a writer say: "This character just won't behave himself. I meant him to do this and that, and instead he keeps doing something quite different." It's also common for a minor character to take over a scene or even a whole play, emerging into far greater prominence than you had ever intended.

Perhaps this all seems rather terrifying. I'm sure you would feel more secure if you thought that everything could be kept firmly under your control. But that isn't how it works in practice.

The creation of characters comes about partly by design and partly as a result of an unconscious process which you will gradually learn to trust.

I see the first stage as a sort of fertilisation. Something already present in your imagination fuses with a particular stimulus; perhaps it's a specific person you see, meet or hear about. From that embryo the character begins to grow. You may make some conscious decisions about certain aspects but others will apparently emerge of their own accord. Gradually, what at first existed only as a germ of an idea begins to take on more and more characteristics of a living, multi-faceted human being, till eventually your character is ready to speak, walk off the page and breathe with an autonomous life of her own.

As your characters begin to come to life they will become more like people you know than people you have created. Since your ultimate aim is to introduce them to your audience as full-blooded human beings this is obviously all to the good. But as they separate themselves from you you may experience surprisingly strong reactions to them. This character, you decide, is someone you like, trust and admire whereas that one doesn't appeal to you at all. I regularly fall violently in love with certain characters whilst experiencing considerable difficulty in coming to terms with the behaviour and habits of others.

I've found it useful to try to practise a measure of equanimity towards my creations, looking for the more negative or unattractive aspects of those who most appeal to me, and attempting to extend compassion towards those who seem most unappealing.

It's important not to be judgemental about your characters. Your task is to present them, trying not to pre-empt the audience's reaction. In any case, if your villains are unremittingly villainous they will come across as stereotypes, as subtle as the Ugly Sisters, and probably only half as humorous.

Similarly, it's hard for the audience to empathise with a character who is wholly good, totally without fault. If you think about even the most delightful person you know, you can probably quickly detect a few minor flaws in their perfection.

One of the ways in which theatre can actually improve on life is that it offers the opportunity to view characters at more than one level at a time. It's a little like one of those bottles filled with layers of multi-coloured sand, or a cross section taken through a piece of rock to give a view of its many strata at one glance.

David Lan, in his play *Flight,* explores this possibility. The play deals with events in the life of a family of affluent and somewhat complacent South African Jews. Our view of them would be very different were it not for the author's use of a very simple device which permits the past to invade the present. Whilst following the fortunes of the characters in the present we are also able to watch them at key points in their past, thus learning how they had come to the country as poor, but radical immigrants, driven out of Europe by the pogroms. This insight into the history of the people on the stage obviously affects our reaction to them, offering both mitigation and ironic commentary on their present behaviour.

Shamrocks and Crocodiles by Heidi Thomas deals with events following the suicide of Eddie Massey, described as a 'bankrupt Dublin-born immigrant to Liverpool'. Moving easily between the present and the past, Thomas allows her characters, Christine and Dominic, to appear both in the present, aged 19 and 18 respectively, and as their childhood selves, as seen in the following sequence:

DOMINIC   What you drawing?
CHRISTINE A picture
DOMINIC   What of?
CHRISTINE A person.
DOMINIC   Who?
CHRISTINE God.
DOMINIC   God's not a person. And nobody knows what he looks like.
CHRISTINE Well? They will when this is finished. Anyway, Uncle Frank says God looks like Ronnie Drew out of the Dubliners.
DOMINIC   God wasn't Irish. He was a Jew.
CHRISTINE He had a beard.
DOMINIC   He never sang in a band.
                   (THE ARGUMENT STOPS SHORT AS CHRISTINE FIXES DOMINIC WITH A COLD, SPITEFUL STARE. SLOWLY AT FIRST, AND THEN WITH INCREASING SPEED AND VIOLENCE, SHE DRAGS HER PENCIL BACK AND FORTH ACROSS THE PAGE UNTIL THE DRAWING IS COVERED WITH SCRIBBLE.)
CHRISTINE There. Now it is utterly and completely ruined.
                   (DRAMATICALLY, BITTERLY, SHE SCREWS UP THE PAPER AND THROWS IT ON THE FLOOR. DOMINIC CAPERS ABOUT IN HIGH DELIGHT, MOCKING HIS SISTER'S MANNERISMS AND VOICE.)
DOMINIC   "Utterly and completely ruined! Utterly and completely ruined!"

The tension and the gaps between the external and internal aspects of your character are a strong basis for conflict out of which drama can develop. Similarly, the interaction between characters at various levels of their unconscious, as well as in their more obvious and overt behaviour, will also provide you with a great deal of potential material.

Peter Nichols, in *Passion Play,* makes specific reference to the battle between what Jung termed 'sub-personalities': that is, warring aspects within an individual. He actually gives his characters alternative personae who act out the thoughts and desires which most of us keep hidden well below the surface.

Your aim in drawing a character is to be as specific as possible. Generalisation will lead to the creation of stereotypes, not recognisable human beings. Learn to look for the ways in which people differ one from another, and revel in the differences. What quirks, idiosyncrasies, surprising good qualities or unexpected vices distinguish your character from another who is something like her? Stereotypes always insult, since they deprive characters of their individuality.

There is only a thin line between a character who is so wonderfully recognisable that she makes the audience wince or laugh aloud with pleasure at the writer's accuracy and one who is absolutely stereotypical. The difference is that stereotypes are caricatures, crudely drawn with a large brush and an often cynical eye. They seem to say to the audience: "If I draw it this big will you get the point?"

In contrast, your 'recognisable' character is drawn in fine detail, line by delicate line, the picture carefully built up with light and shade. You don't assault the audience, rather invite them to discover a common bond, to enjoy that empathy, to explore it and learn from it.

If your characters are based on real people, ie people you have actually met, seen and heard, you obviously have a head start as far as realistic detail is concerned. This is where you will find it necessary to select and shape the information available to you. Don't forget, you are the only person who has the complete picture. You can offer the audience as much or as little as you wish, selecting what will be most revealing to communicate the story you have to tell.

I have already mentioned *Iron Them Dry,* one of the plays written during the first 'Made in Wales' workshop. The play was totally autobiographical and the characters depicted were all based on real people. The main characters, though given fictitious names, were Pat (the writer), seen from childhood through to her wedding day, and her mother and father.

At first Pat was reluctant to omit any detail at all in her characterisation. It was very important to her, in those early stages, to depict things exactly as they had been. Given the deeply emotive nature of the whole experience, I was reluctant to impose or even suggest any deviation from the facts. Later, as she began to distance herself from the subject, and particularly once she had had the experience of finishing two drafts, she began to see for herself how she could distil experience and extrapolate from it, offering the audience not an exact blow-by-blow account but the essence of events, without in any way sacrificing authenticity.

In the same way, as she developed more confidence in her craft as a writer, she was able to see the possibility in characterisation of relinquishing certain details and accentuating others, whilst not losing sight of her original intention to portray real events and people as truthfully as possible.

Remember: theatre is magic and you are the magician. You can conjure characters out of thin air; the rules, if there are any, are only there to be broken.

Since all the characters are your inventions a whole range of possibilities is open to you. Real people can mingle with fictitious people. People from the past can rub shoulders with characters from the present or future. Characters from fiction can converse with characters from history.

Caryl Churchill enjoys and explores this freedom in the first act of *Top Girls,* where a group of women gather round a table in a glossy London restaurant to help Marlene, her fictitious modern high flyer, to celebrate a recent promotion. The guests are as follows: Isabella Bird (a Victorian explorer), Lady Nijo (an Emperor's concubine from 13th-Century Japan), Dull Gret (the subject of a Brueghel painting which depicts a woman charging through hell and fighting the demons), Pope Joan (who, disguised as a man, is thought to have held office in the 9th Century) and Patient Griselda (the obedient wife, whose story is told by Chaucer in 'The Clerk's Tale'.) Churchill offers no explanation whatsoever for the presence of such a mixed bunch. In the setting she has devised for them the women experience no difficulty in communicating with each other, with Marlene, and with the audience. It is a daring and innovative device that crosses boundaries of logic and rationality to explore the common experiences of a wildly diverse group of women.

The fact that the characters can speak to each other at all, sharing painful memories as well as jokes, communicates strongly to a modern audience. It is a tribute to the author's wit and skill, but it is also excellent proof that, in the theatre, practically anything can be made credible provided it is presented with sufficient conviction and panache.

Don't, however, make the mistake of thinking that, if you base your characters on historical figures or characters famous in literature, you will avoid the problems involved in creating people purely in your imagination.

In many ways it's harder to make a real person come convincingly to life than it is to create a character from scratch. It's all too easy to be mesmerised by your subject's fame or greatness or to become bewildered by a mass of research and conflicting information.

Unless the character comes alive for you, existing in your imagination with a distinctive personality and voice, there is little hope that she will live for the audience, however familiar they may be with her history. A mass of factual information is not sufficient to make a character breathe. We need to sense hidden feelings, as well as be told obvious truths, to empathise with her inner conflicts, hopes, desires, doubts and fears. If history books provide no real clues or food for thought, then close them and rely on your own imagination and don't feel daunted by what you have been told. Allow the character to come alive without further reference to received information. After all, we have no infallible way of knowing characters from the past, so your imaginings are as valid and as worthy of consideration as any one else's. There is, anyway, no such thing as historical fact, only a series of often conflicting opinions.

Peter Shaffer, in *Amadeus*, creates a complex study of jealousy and remorse in the character of Salieri, Mozart's contemporary and rival. His unflattering if amusing depiction of Mozart himself may owe less to historical fact than to his own imagination yet we are quite prepared to believe and accept what is laid before us.

When the writer feels constrained by historical detail or has a sense of more learned scholars breathing down her neck, the result is usually a play that is pedestrian and unchallenging, with characters who, though superficially recognisable, are wooden and lifeless.

How can you decide what characters are needed to tell your story? Like most aspects of playwriting, the answer lies in a mixture of instinct and craft.

You could perhaps begin by identifying your protagonist, ie the character who seems to you to be the main focus. This is the person in whom the audience will take the most interest, with whom they will most strongly identify and whose actions will provide the thread which draws them through the play from start to finish.

This character will probably have an opponent or antagonist. This is someone who sets off a reaction, who provokes conflict by blocking the protagonist's desires. The two may be engaged in direct conflict or simply indulging in a subtle or delicate battle of wits but the opposition will be there and out of that opposition drama will grow.

In Sartre's classic play, *Huis Clos* (sometimes translated as *Vicious Circle*), this juxtaposition of characters is seen in its most undiluted form. The bleak and enclosed room, which is the writer's vision of hell, houses three deliberately ill-matched people: Estelle, the selfish and beautiful socialite who murdered her own child; Ines, a lesbian, who desires her; and Garcin, who died a coward. This choice of characters is precisely calculated to evoke the maximum degree of conflict between them. There is no way they can occupy their claustrophobic prison without causing pain to each other.

The play is deliberately simplistic. Sartre's main intention was to illustrate the maxim: "Hell is other people." There is no main protagonist. Instead, the three characters interweave in a deadly and repetitive dance from which they have no hope of escape. It's hard to empathise with any of them since, in order to drive the message home, the writer actually exaggerates the negative aspects of their personalities almost to the point of caricature.

Nevertheless, the play does provide a useful illustration, since it highlights the reasons why a writer might choose one character rather than another; Sartre's choice of these three is deliberately calculated to produce a very particular effect.

In the workshops I encouraged the students to answer the question: "Why these people?". What is it about the juxtaposition of these particular people which will produce conflict and therefore drama?

It's not enough to put two characters on the stage and make them have an argument. To work from Mamet's proposition, there must be something within each of them which will inevitably spark off a reaction in the other, out of which conflict will develop and need to be resolved, and which will lead to what comes to be seen as an inevitable conclusion.

It is this conflict between characters, and within characters, which will propel your play forward, speech by speech, scene by scene, providing the mainspring of the action.

Characters who are multi-faceted, full of contradictions and inner turmoil, obviously have far greater dramatic potential than those who are drawn without subtlety. Similarly, the more you can differentiate between characters the more possibilities of dramatic developments you will discover in their interaction.

I know that inexperienced writers find it hard to make characters who are distinct from each other, who sound different, and who act in distinctive ways. A useful guideline is to ask yourself some questions about status and role.

In any group of people, whether long-established or random, a pecking order will quickly emerge. There will be those who consider themselves high status, whether by reason of class, profession, personal psychology or a combination of factors, and who act accordingly. High status people demand special treatment, expect concessions or deference from others. Low status people defer to others, acting apologetically, displaying humility or signs of oppression. Sometimes a person may give himself a higher status than that accorded by the group; sometimes the reverse is true.

As you begin to collect your intended characters ask yourself who has the highest status amongst them and who the lowest. Would there be a level of consensus about the relative status of the characters or are there those whose self-esteem is higher or lower than it should be?

Similarly, in any group such as a family, a group of colleagues at work, or even a random grouping of people travelling on the same bus or drinking in the same bar, relative status may be clearly defined and, as a result, roles assumed or assigned.

The gap between assumed and assigned status is a rich source of conflict that may give rise to developments which can be either comic or tragic. Confusion over status or role can be actively used as a dramatic device. The pantomime *Cinderella* is a classic example of this technique. Dandini and the Prince change roles; thus Dandini, the valet, is automatically assigned a higher status in the village. Confusion arises when people respond to the role he is playing. Cinderella believes he *is* the Prince and that the man she loves is the valet. Similarly, Cinderella's lowly status is reversed when the fairy godmother dresses her in finery and sends her to the ball, where the Prince mistakes her for a princess.

Many plays by Shakespeare are also based on similar confusions: women dressed as men, royalty masquerading as commoners. The drama derives from the mixed messages this produces. When Olivia falls in love with Viola, dressed as a boy, in *Twelfth Night,* does she love a woman or a man?

Drama is also inherent in the situation where a character breaks out of the role assigned to her by her friends, family or society. Rita, in Willy Russell's *Educating Rita* and Beattie in Arnold Wesker's *Roots* are both good examples of this phenomenon.

The gap between how a person perceives herself and how she is perceived by others provides another fruitful breeding ground for conflict. The jostling for position within a group creates conflict. The frustration of hopes of improving status or changing roles creates conflict. A loss of status, and what that reveals in terms of people's changed reactions, may create tragedy as in *King Lear.*

To explore this more fully it may prove helpful to imagine your characters outside the context of your intended play. If they were shipwrecked on an island who would take charge? Who would panic? Who would remain calm? If the master were to become the servant, or vice-versa, who would command the more respect? If you met your hero at a party would you enjoy his company or would he bore you stiff?

If you saw your characters walking down the street which one would you notice first?

Perhaps you are already beginning to wonder what all these people should be called. Names for characters are important and should be given serious thought. Names go in and out of fashion, differ from region to region and according to social class. If your character is a woman in her 70's it is unlikely that she would be called Tracey or Kylie. Unless, of course, there is a bizarre explanation: perhaps she has recently changed her name or is masquerading as a twenty-year-old, or is an ardent fan of Australian soap opera. These considerations aside, she is more likely to be called Daisy or Blanche; if she is the daughter of Jewish immigrants you might opt for Zelda or Esther.

Names suggest characteristics. John sounds solid, reliable and ordinary. Lance sounds more daring and dashing. Tizzy, Lizzie and Dizzie sound girlish, a little wild perhaps; Gertrude and Margaret will probably be more sober, older, more conventional.

Surnames may be chosen either for regional resonance (the telephone directory is a valuable reference book) or because they too evoke certain characteristics.

John Woodman sounds a solid sort of bloke, but Peter Flack could be looking for bother. I couldn't think of a name for a wild young girl in my play *Bardo* till I suddenly decided she must be called 'Magpie', because, in the words of another character, "she takes things". I called the main character 'Jack Mansfield', a name I chose because I thought it sounded as if he might be almost anybody.

Occupations, too, are important. Sometimes, of course, the occupation of a character is dictated by the story, or may even be the focus of it. In other cases you are in the position of having to choose a particular occupation.

If you want a character to be a brain surgeon or a deep sea diver don't be put off by your lack of specialist knowledge on the subject. Though action research may be impossible, you can probably find out all you need to know by interviewing practitioners and reading whatever first-hand accounts you can find.

What a person does for a living will occupy a great deal of time and energy and will therefore be a major influence on behaviour and outlook. Tension between professional and home life, dissatisfaction with career, frustrated ambitions, conflict in the workplace — all these are potential sources of dramatic tension.

If you have specialised knowledge of a fascinating work environment, then why not draw on it for raw material? Audiences love to be allowed to see behind the scenes. Arnold Wesker, in *The Kitchen*, sets his play in the hectic and colourful world he inhabited when he worked in the kitchens of a smart hotel. In *Chips With Everything* he draws on his personal knowledge of life in the R.A.F. and in *The Journalists* reveals the inner workings of the world of newspapers, another environment with which he is very familiar. It's always fascinating to watch people at work on stage, to see in detail the nuts and bolts of what they actually do. In my play *The Ballad of Tilly Hake* there are several work scenes. In one we see gleaners in the fields; in another sequence we watch a woman preparing reed to be used for thatching. The actors used genuine implements and had to learn to carry out the work as they would in real life.

In the original production of *The Contractor* by David Storey a marquee was actually erected on stage in the course of the action, whilst Michael Frayn's *Noises Off* takes us backstage to witness what the audience never sees behind the scenes of a production mounted by an inept theatre company.

Ask yourself questions about your character's occupation. Does it confer status? Does it give satisfaction? Does it induce pressure, produce conflict? Sometimes a whole play can revolve around the answer to such enquiries, as in David Mamet's *Glengarry Glen Ross*, which deals with the appalling pressures of life in the American real estate business. The breakneck speed of the action mirrors the incredible pace of life in a cut-throat world.

A problem for many inexperienced playwrights is how to allow characters to speak for themselves. There is always a great temptation to make characters into mouthpieces for your own pet preoccupations and hobby-horses. The result is not individuals or living people but a set of puppets who are all remarkably similar and who all bear a marked resemblance to their creator. This is a particular danger in 'issue' plays, which deal overtly with a social or political topic that the writer wishes to expose, analyse or explore. But here, as elsewhere, your aim should be not to speak through your characters but to let your characters speak for themselves. Allow them to be who they are and to say what comes naturally to them rather than force-feeding them with pre-packaged speeches. Your point of view will emerge just as clearly but with greater subtlety; an audience may have no objection to gentle persuasion but will resent being assaulted by your viewpoint.

The characters in your play will evolve through a process which is as mysterious as the emergence of the first idea. Nevertheless, you will need to make some conscious decisions. A very important question to ask is: "How does this character speak?"

Your research should prove helpful. If you have learnt to keep your ears as well as your eyes open you will have observed that every person has a very distinctive and individual way of speaking. This involves use of vocabulary, sentence structure, delivery — fast, slow, loud, soft, staccato, etc. Some people speak with a particular regional accent or local vernacular. Professor Higgins claimed he could place a person to the very street by the way he spoke. You may not need to be quite as particular but you will need to consider the many factors which influence speech. Origins, education, class, status, self-image, role, intention, psychology, state of mind all play a part in determining what is said and how it is spoken.

There are, of course, infinite subtleties of speech, just as there are of appearance. Just as you may ask, on *seeing* a person: "Who do you want me to think you are?", the same question arises the first time you hear someone speak.

Are accent, vocabulary or syntax deliberately used to mislead the listener, to give a false impression or does the speaker inadvertently reveal fear, doubt or duplicity through hesitation, unfinished sentences, repetition or self justification?

Your aim as a playwright is to establish each character with a distinct and quite unmistakeable voice. Once a character is introduced it should be possible to know who is speaking without consulting the names in the margin, because each character speaks in a voice which is sharply differentiated from all the others.

The first time a character appears is very important to an audience. It's a little like first impressions in real life. The audience will glean a great deal of information from how a character looks on his first entrance, what he says and how he says it, and how he engages with the other characters on the stage.

Heidi Thomas introduces her two main characters in the second scene of *Indigo*, the story of an African prince and the son of a Liverpudlian slave merchant. First, Ide, the African:

IDE   When I was a child I used to watch my brother dancing. The dust was hot and yellow then, burning under the drum-loud trees, as high as the humming woodsmoke. Pink-heeled and panting, he kicked at the sand as he sang. It was a song of clouds and fishes, birds and stone — a lisping tongue libation to the magic gods. He was eight years old; vivid with oyster beads, noisy as a village and as rich as paint. A string of joy stirred my voice from my belly. "I love you, Ibike!" I cried. He kept on dancing. He rattled his beasts' cream bones. He was reciting spells and incantations; for the world was pressing on him and he had no time to waste on little children such as I.

Then William, the Englishman, speaks:

WILLIAM   My father would never look up at me when I went into his workshop. "William," he would say. That was all. I stood in my infant's pinafore, figurehead still, watching him work by candlelight, under the beat of rain. I saw him pulling and weaving, his horned hands darting through the pale blond hemp. Bleached grass and dead green blossoms, coiled into headless serpents wound on wood. "What are you doing?" I said one day. "I'm making rope." I heard the seagulls sounding, blue-voiced and thin in the dockside air. "Rope for the boats?" He nodded. I smelt the sea and saw the rope stretched gut-thin and golden in the salted sky. Catching the wind in a hobby-horse harness, riding the grey-white waves on a saddle of ship. "When I am a man will I be a ropemaker?" His eyes were dark, like plums in twilight. "Nay, lad. There'll be better than the likes of this for thee . . . "

Characters don't actually need to say a great deal to reveal themselves. Sometimes their limited or impoverished speech is the main clue to who they are. Steve Gooch, at the beginning of *Mister Fun,* a play set in a fairground, introduces us to four young people. He first describes them as follows:

> THEY (GIL AND MARSHY) HOLD THE POLES OF THEIR TWO DODGEM CARS AND WATCH THE PUNTERS. SHELLEY AND WINA STAND ON THE EDGE OF THE RINK.

MARSHY   Bit thin, en't it?
GIL   I reckon they're still in hibernation.
MARSHY   Not much talent.
GIL   An' what there is, I wouldn't touch with yours.
MARSHY   (SNICKERS) Hoo. (PAUSE) 'ey, who's that with Shelley? I could go for her.
GIL   What, for life? Or with a knife?
MARSHY   What —? (REALISES) Oh. (SNICKERS)
GIL   Only dip your bread in the best gravy, my dad used to say. Or you lose your sense of taste.
MARSHY   Wha—? Oh. (SNICKERS)

Both characters are quickly defined in this brief exchange, with Gil established as the greater wit, possibly the ring-leader, and Marshy struggling to keep up. Very little is said yet Gooch tells us unequivocally who these boys are, what they are doing and hints at the relationship between them.

The character Dull Gret in *Top Girls* has a distinctive and idiosyncratic vocabulary and mode of expression, made all the more striking by the fact that for much of the first act she concentrates on eating and leaves conversation to her companions. When she does speak her voice is unmistakeable:

GRET: We come into hell through a big mouth. Hell's black and red. It's like the
         village where I come from. There's a river and a bridge and houses.
         There's places on fire like when the soldiers come. There's a big devil
         sat on a roof with a big hole in his arse and he's scooping stuff out of it
         with a big ladle and it's falling down on us, and it's money, so a lot of the
         women stop and get some. But most of us is fighting the devils. There's
         lots of little devils, our size, and we get them down all right and give
         them a beating. There's a lot of funny creatures round your feet, you
         don't like to look, like rats and lizards, and nasty things, a bum with a
         face, and fish with legs, and faces on things that don't have faces on. But
         they don't hurt, you just keep going. Well, we'd had worse, you see,
         we'd had the Spanish. We'd all had family killed. Men on wheels. Babies
         on swords. I'd had enough. I was mad. I hate the bastards. I come out
         my front door that morning and shout till my neighbours come out and
         I said:– "Come on, we're going where the evil come from and pay the
         bastards out".

A true ear for dialogue is very much like an ear for music or a photographic
memory. Some people have a natural aptitude, some don't. Clearly, if you
fall into the first category, you are at a distinct advantage. But you can
train yourself to improve your ear simply by listening to how people speak
and by asking yourself questions about what their speech reveals or
conceals. Do they use words to build themselves up or to pull themselves
down, to reveal themselves or as a shield to hide behind?

Don't fall into the trap of patronising less articulate characters by never
allowing them a flight of fancy, a sudden outburst of poetry, ecstasy or
wild humour. People don't always speak in the same way. Circumstances
alter and speech may change to accommodate the difference. Even the
most unimaginative or apparently leaden character may have access to
metaphor or heightened forms of expression when specifically moved or
excited by events. Although he may only ever express himself in
unsophisticated language and a narrow range of imagery he must still be
capable of indicating, in his own fashion, how strongly he feels about
something or how deeply it has moved him.

The emotion pushes the language through to a sudden and unexpected
articulacy. So Lindsay in *Free 'n' Lovely,* my play about a seedy beauty
contest, describes her vision of a better life:

"I saw this programme about breeding cats. Russian Blues they was
called. Big blue eyes they had . . . thick fur like velvet. This woman who
bred them lived in a big house in the middle of the New Forest. I mean,
when I say big, there was enough room for about 25 kids . . . a ruddy

great staircase going right up the middle, like you see in the old films . . . carpets everywhere . . . silver candlesticks . . . different cups and saucers for breakfast and tea . . . enough plates for a wedding. She had horses too . . . four of them. Plenty of room for them to run about. It was like . . . it was like one of them posh calendars. November . . . horses standing around under the trees . . . frost on the ground . . . the sun in the sky all sort of orange and rusty looking."

Believable dialogue is not necessarily always an exact replica of everyday speech. While it takes its flavour from the authentic rhythms, cadences and vocabulary of words overheard and remembered, the words are arranged by the writer so as to have the maximum impact, to make the strongest possible statement about the character.

Listen to Barrie Keeffe's football fan in *Abide With Me*. The action takes place on Cup Final Day.

"They'll barricade the windows, the pubs'll lock their doors, the lights will go off in the shops and the police will line the pavements, white with fear . . . cops' hats'll bobble like decorations on a windy promenade . . . the air will be heavy with shouts and yells and the smashing of glass . . . No one will ignore us – We will not be ignored. They'll talk about us, write about us, hate us. Hate us. Hate us. Animals, call us animals . . . not ignore me . . . won't be ignored . . . not ignore me . . . not . . . ignore . . . me."

He speaks with a kind of heightened awareness which veers towards poetry. Though his choice of words may seem strongly reminiscent of many similar outbursts, Keeffe has deliberately organised and designed the speech for maximum effect on the audience.

Caryl Churchill is a writer who has experimented with new ways of actually arranging dialogue on the page so as to capture most effectively the interruptions, hiatuses and cross-talking which characterise everyday speech. A study of the text of *Top Girls* or *Icecream*, a more recent play, will illustrate how her system works. She explains it in the introductory notes to *Top Girls*:

A speech usually follows the one immediately before it BUT:–
1) When one character starts speaking before the other has finished, the point of interruption is marked /
2) A character sometimes continues speaking right through another's speech.
3) Sometimes a speech follows on from a speech earlier than the one immediately before it, and continuity is marked*.

Perhaps you don't yet feel confident enough to juggle with technical innovations but it is nevertheless worth noting that there are no hard and fast rules. If you feel that your play demands an entirely new approach to dialogue then you must invent it, just as Churchill did. Perhaps you want all your characters to speak at once; perhaps speeches are to be delivered in a round. Perhaps you need to mix contemporary speech with a form of expression which evokes another age, past or future. Perhaps one of your characters speaks in a foreign language or an invented language, or doesn't speak at all.

It's also worth remembering that people don't always tell the truth. A person may lie to defend herself, to save face, to avert a crisis, or to give a deliberately false impression of her status. Look at this speech, again from *Top Girls*. Shona is being interviewed by Nell for a top job which she desperately wants.

NELL   So just fill me in a bit more could you about what you've been doing.

SHONA   What I've been doing. It's all down there.

NELL   The bare facts are down here but I've got to present you to an employer.

SHONA   I'm twenty-nine years old.

NELL   So it says here.

SHONA   We look young. Youngness runs in the family in our family.

NELL   So just describe your present job for me.

SHONA   My present job at present. I have a car. I have a Porsche. I go up the M1 a lot. Burn up the M1 a lot. Straight up the M1 in the fast lane to where the clients are, Staffordshire, Yorkshire, I do a lot in Yorkshire. I'm selling electric things. Like dishwashers, washing machines, stainless steel tubs are a feature and the reliability of the programme. After sales service, we offer a very good after sales service, spare parts, plenty of spare parts. And fridges, I sell a lot of fridges, specially in the summer, people want to buy fridges in the summer because of the heat melting the butter and you get fed up standing the milk in a basin of cold water with a cloth over, stands to reason people don't want to do that in this day and age. So I sell a lot of them. Big ones with big freezers. Big freezers. And I stay in hotels at night when I'm away from home. On my expense account. I stay in various hotels. They know me, the ones I go to. I check in, have a bath, have a shower. Then I go down to the bar, have a gin and tonic, have a chat. Then I go into the dining room and have dinner. I usually have fillet steak and mushrooms. I like mushrooms. I like smoked salmon very much. I like having a salad on the side. Green salad. I don't like tomatoes.

NELL   Christ, what a waste of time.

SHONA   Beg your pardon?
NELL   Not a word of this is true is it.

Don't forget the power of silence. It's not necessary for your characters to talk all the time, to explain everything, to describe everything. Sometimes, as both Pinter and Beckett demonstrate, few words or no words at all reveal more than continuous dialogue. What people omit to say is often more potent.

You will start with a vague general idea for your character, a little like a blurred photograph or a rough sketch. Then gradually you will bring the picture into sharper and sharper focus. The fine points begin to emerge, the many subtle shades of colour. Your character acquires a walk, some clothes, a distinctive voice, a history, perhaps a family, a profession, friends, enemies, hopes, frustrations. An idea is gradually transformed into flesh and blood.

How do you decide how many characters there should be in your play? The first question is: "How many do you need?" What characters are necessary to move the action forward, to tell the story? Every character must have a distinct and vital function. There should be no maids with messages unless those maids also have a biography and a further role in the story. There should be no spear-carriers unless you are hoping to explore the life of a spear-carrier, his conflicts, his ambitions, his desires.

It's partly a matter of pure economics. Since your ultimate aim in writing a play is to see it produced on the stage then it may be worth remembering that, in a professional production, every character represents a salary to be paid. Sometimes it's possible for several parts to be played by the same actor but even then there is no place for characters who have no function in the plot.

Of course, there are plays with a cast of a hundred or more, for example the community play, as pioneered by Ann Jellicoe and the Colway Theatre Trust.

Here the writer has a special and probably unique brief to create a cast of around 180 so that as many local people as possible may enjoy participating. Such a project is possible because the actors are amateurs and receive no salary. Even so, a writer cannot create 180 fully drawn characters, neither can the audience identify strongly with that number. So, what actually happens is that the writer invents a relatively small number of main characters (say 10 or 12), whose biographies are well developed and who have a focal role in the unfolding of the action. There is then a larger number of smaller roles. These are characters who may not have a great deal to say although they feature prominently in the action.

The rest of the characters are virtually 'crowd'. The writer should still give each character a credible, if sketchy, biography and, if possible, a brief moment of glory in the action. No actor, whether amateur or professional, can portray a cipher.

It's probably better for an inexperienced writer to start by creating three characters and to attempt to draw them as subtly and in as fine detail as possible than to create five, only to encounter problems in differentiating between them or giving each a strong enough function in the story.

It's hard enough to juggle dialogue between three characters and to ensure that one does not disappear from a scene whilst the other two engage in spirited discussion. The more characters you introduce the more care you must take to ensure that each has a 'story' to follow through the play. An actor, bewildered in rehearsal, will often say she is searching for a 'through line', the thread which draws her through the play, scene by scene, from start to finish.

Once a play is cast, actors are naturally most interested in the activities, motivation and speeches of their own character. Sometimes a writer will inadvertently allow a character to drop out of the plot. You may not notice this omission but the actor who has to play the part most certainly will, demanding either a logical explanation or a more satisfactory slice of the action.

Probably the most important thing to remember as you work on the creation of your imaginary characters is that each one will need to convince the actor that she is a real person. An actor can't easily play a cardboard cut-out.

If you want the audience to believe in your characters, to empathise with them, to follow their fortunes and care about the outcome of their actions, they will need to be as subtle, as complex, as flawed and as unpredictable as we all are. They will be as capable of passion, despair, duplicity, heroism, viciousness, anger, lust, pettiness, jealousy, cruelty, ecstasy, as each member of the audience. They will not be black and white villains or heroes. A villain is not a villain to his mother, or in his own mind: he is maligned and misunderstood; he is misguided, under severe pressure, prone to unaccountable outbursts of bad behaviour. A hero may be desperately insecure, bluffing to appear brave, insensitive to his children, subject to melancholia, plagued by unhappy memories, cruel to his cats.

Nor should you think of your characters as static embodiments of 'greed', 'anger', 'lust', etc. like those in a medieval morality play. People can and do change and it is this potential within individual characters or in the relationship between them which can be the mainspring of action in your play.

Audiences want to be convinced but they also love to be surprised, to see events take an unexpected turn. They enjoy seeing the people on stage do things they have dreamed of doing, but never dared, or things they *have* done, but only in secret. They are, in fact, inclined to believe that the characters on stage are real people, at least for the duration of the play. They will willingly subscribe to this fantasy if you will only give them sufficient help.

Audiences come to the theatre to be transported, to enter the world you have devised for them. They are therefore prepared to laugh or cry and become totally involved. Your job, as a playwright, is to enable this to happen. Your power, as a playwright, is that, when the magic really works, you can play the audience like a finely tuned instrument, to evoke any response you wish.

Project: Creating a character

GO TO A CROWDED PLACE

▷ Choose a busy shopping centre, a large store or a bus station and then:
    a) Pick out one person to observe.
    b) Absorb as much as you can about that person's external appearance: clothes, hair, facial expression, walk, manner, etc.
    c) Ask yourself: "Who do you want me to think you are?"
    d) Write a one-page description of your character in as much detail as possible. Be particular rather than general.

DEVELOP THE CHARACTER

▷ Write an internal monologue for your character, exploring her/his thoughts, dreams, fears, hopes. Try to extrapolate from what you have observed. Account for anything odd or striking, eg a heavy coat worn in warm weather, worn shoes, etc.

▷ Now write a monologue for the same character but imagine that she/

he is addressing someone else who does not interrupt. Think about:

    a) Speech rhythms, syntax and vocabulary.

    b) Accent and/or dialect.

    c) The role and status of the other, silent, character.

▷ Create two characters and then:

    a) Write a page of dialogue in which one character describes a personal experience to the other.

    b) Write a page of dialogue in which the two characters discuss someone they both know.

    c) Write a page of dialogue in which one character is lying to the other.

CHAPTER FIVE

Structure, Form and Style –
Breaking the Rules

– The classic structure – Playing with time –
– Fantasy and the real world – The play within a play –
– Writing a monologue – The epic play – Surreal theatre –
– The schematic approach – The organic approach –
– What is dramatic? – Plotting –
– The sub-plot – The starting point –
– The arrival of the stranger – Settings –
– The location as metaphor – Endings – The signalling device –
– **Project: Developing a story** –

Writing a play is like building a house single-handed. First you need a basic idea, a rough mental picture of the sort of house you want. Where will it be situated? How many people will live in it? Do you see a grand building with ten bedrooms, a long curving driveway and marble pillars? Or a simple cottage, economic and functional? Or perhaps you dream of a rambling, chaotic mansion, one room leading into another, with mysterious nooks and crannies, surprising cupboards and a startling view of the sea . . .

You begin to draw up detailed plans. You collect all your raw materials; you dig the foundations. The scaffolding goes up; the pipes are laid . . . work is under way.

Then, one glorious day, all the work is finished. No more piles of sand, no more cement-mixers. Gone is the scaffolding, the jumble of exposed wires. What you see may not be precisely what you visualised in your mind's eye. But it's *your* house nevertheless, with windows that open and close, with walls and ceilings, stairs and doors.

The structure of your play is like the scaffolding used whilst building work is in progress — essential during the construction phase but never intended to form a visible part of the finished product. The form is what you actually see: the house itself, giving little or no hint of the many processes involved in its construction.

Sometimes a play is criticised as being too schematic. What this means is that, although the house is apparently finished, the scaffolding is still left standing, the gas pipes are still exposed as though they were a special feature of the design. How your play has been built is your secret. What the audience sees, the form, the finished article, should be something which strikes them as harmonious, good to look at, appropriate to its purpose. They have no need to know how that effect has been achieved.

Another analogy is to think of the structure as the skeleton. When the audience watch your play they don't have x-ray vision. We may have a knowledge of the anatomy of theatre and so be conscious of what lies beneath the skin but we have no desire to see it. In fact, if we are made to feel too aware of the mechanics of your writing it will probably interfere with our enjoyment and involvement.

There is a classic structure for a play just as there is a classic design for a house. But not every story lends itself to being told in the same way. The right structure for your play will liberate your ideas; the wrong structure will constrain them.

You have something of importance to say. Your main aim should be to discover the most effective way of saying it. Your search for an appropriate and liberating structure is simply a search for a way of arranging your material which will allow you to communicate your ideas most powerfully.

Women's plays have often been attacked as being defective in structure, a statement which says as much about the critic as the subject of his criticism. What is actually being said is that the work doesn't obey the perceived and hitherto accepted rules regarding the 'proper' construction of a play. This may be because the writer, finding established rules and models a constraint, has unconsciously (or perhaps even consciously) invented new ones to accommodate ideas and ways of looking at the world which cannot easily be expressed in existing forms.

The first step, therefore, is to lose your respect for the whole concept of structure and your awe of all those well-made plays. Instead, why not experiment with various possibilities, searching for the most natural and expressive form for what you have to say.

Perhaps we should begin by looking briefly at the mould which I'm so blithely encouraging you to break. A classic structure could be described as follows:

The play begins with an incident that acts as a trigger. This is followed by complications or developments arising from that incident. One thing leads to another until a crisis point is reached. This crisis has to be

resolved. This will then lead us to the climax and thence to the dénoue-
ment. It's all very straightforward. Perhaps you'd like to try to apply this
framework to a play you know well to see for yourself how it works. Let's
take *Cinderella*.

There are actually *two* trigger incidents: 1. The Baron Hardup and his
daughters are about to be evicted by the bailiffs. 2. The Prince and
Dandini agree to change places. Complications develop from both,
leading to the crisis, which is that Cinderella can't go to the ball. The Fairy
Godmother resolves the crisis with magic. The climax of the piece is the
discovery that the slipper fits, and the dénoument is that the real prince
is revealed, marries Cinderella, rescues her family from penury,
and everyone lives happily ever after. The system works. At least for
Cinderella and the many others to follow in her glass-shod footsteps.

But it may not work for you, or only in part. The first thing to learn
about deconstruction is that you must feel free to take whatever might be
useful from the pile of rubble. You can then incorporate it into your new
structure and throw away whatever seems irrelevant or disfunctional.
Although the classic structure may be constraining if adhered to without
deviation, it may still have some useful features. No need, therefore, to
throw the baby out with the bath-water.

Most of my early plays were built on a very simple and unsophisticated
structure. They often concerned two women talking.

The trigger incident was usually rather contrived. My primary aim was
to place diverse characters in a room and let them air their opposing
views.

In *A Quieter Sort of Battle* the characters are an elderly woman who
has sold her house and the younger professional woman who has bought
it. The incident which sets the action in motion is the non-appearance of
the older woman's son to drive her to his home where she will now live.
This hiatus enables the two women to meet, interact and eventually find
unexpected common ground.

A simple structure handled with skill can be extremely effective. It
places great emphasis on convincing characterisation, economy of words
and action. It demands a basic situation which quickly commands interest
and engages the attention of the audience. Gilly Fraser's taut and
engrossing play, *I Can Give You a Good Time*, contains all these
elements. Two contrasting characters locked in a tense encounter. A
claustrophobic setting. The seeds of conflict. A steady build-up of
tension. The obvious threat of violence. The burning questions . . . what
will happen next? How can this possibly be resolved? The answer is
surprising, shocking, but also strangely inevitable.

Sometimes it takes a radical rethink to lift a play out of the purely conventional into a more exciting and challenging realm. I believe that this is what happened with *Self Portrait*. I had originally conceived of it as being told in flashback. The action was to begin at the end of the story, when Gwen John was brought to the hospice in Dieppe, where she was to die and be buried in an unmarked grave. What followed was a series of scenes depicting the events in her life which had led to this place and this point. The play then came full circle to culminate in her death.

That, in itself, was a departure from the classic structure, but a fairly timid one.

Director Annie Castledine quickly saw how this framework was inhibiting me, giving me no natural opportunity to explore deeper issues implicit in the subject and, in particular, to confront the real relevance of the story in contemporary terms.

She asked me to consider my reasons for writing this play and, in so doing, to discover the real subject behind the apparent one. She asked me to consider what might be the most appropriate setting for a play about an artist. Then, as she put it, I was to "throw it all up in the air and see where it comes down". It came down in a very different place.

The new draft of *Self Portrait* that emerged from this discussion was based on a radically different structure which nevertheless owed more than a little to the original concept. Now the play was set in a modern art gallery at which a retrospective exhibition of Gwen John's work was on show. There was now a story involving modern characters. Gwen John's life was explored in a series of short, almost impressionistic scenes, in which the modern characters became their historical counterparts. Gwen herself 'haunted' the gallery, her presence influencing events without ever intruding on them. All this took place in one all-purpose setting where objects had several functions and could acquire fresh significance from scene to scene. There was no explanation of the merging of past and present, little or no change of costume. Lighting changes and the use of recurring musical motifs combined to evoke atmosphere and facilitate the shifts in time and place.

Shedding its original form as a rather pedestrian dramatic biography, the play emerged as surreal and dream-like. Instead of being marooned in its historical and factual context, the subject acquired more subtle shades of meaning and far greater resonance for a modern audience. In the first draft the structure actively prevented me from exploring my real subject; in the second it enabled me to do so. Although the audience needed to work hard to make sense of the whole, they seemed very willing to do this, even enjoying the challenge.

Juggling with time isn't a new concept in dramatic structure. J.B. Priestley used it to great effect in *Time and the Conways* and similar plays. In *Dangerous Corner,* for example, he moves the action forward to a certain point and begins to develop it along increasingly tragic lines. Then he returns to the same point in the action to show what would have happened if the dangerous moment had been averted, if the 'dangerous corner' had been successfully navigated. The outcome is quite different.

You can play with the concept of time in a variety of ways. Perhaps you will decide to tell the story in reverse order, starting with the climax and then showing how events led to that point. In this case the audience will be encouraged to ask not *what* happens next, but *why* it happens and how.

Past and present can co-exist quite happily on the stage, as in *Flight* by David Lan, where events from the past are cut into the narrative to inform and enrich our understanding of the present. The structure is actually similar to that of *Self Portrait.* The continuous story is in present time but this is punctuated by a series of brief interludes which gradually add a further dimension to our knowledge of the characters.

Mooncalf by Roger Stennett is a fantasy for twenty-three actors set on the island of Gruniard. Past, present and fiction combine, unified by the character of Caliban, who, to increase the air of unreality, speaks in an invented language. Figures from Shakespeare's *The Tempest* interweave with modern characters to create a strange and disorientating atmosphere.

You could use the same device to project into the future; alternatively, past, present and future could all be explored simultaneously. Or one character might go back or forward in time, whilst all the others remain in the present.

Don't worry too much about logic or probability. *Alice, After Wonderland,* one play in my one-woman show, *Alice and Other Reflections*, shows Alice in Wonderland as an elderly woman. There's no need to explain how a fictional character can possibly grow old. The Alice we see is an old woman living alone but still dreaming of Wonderland. Outside her room is the real world, with which she seems to have very little contact. Yet she has lived through all the events — including two world wars — which have taken place since Carroll first invented her. The story of 'Wonderland' underpins the piece as she relives the bizarre happenings, after she "fell through a hole in the earth's surface". The action takes place in one room, indeed around one table everlastingly set for tea. The action is one long continuum, a blend of memories and apparently random observations on present and past events. The structure is as illogical as a dream. Past, present, fact and fiction form a collage of impressions. The play gives no answers, simply poses a number of questions.

The 'play within a play' is a form which has been useful to many writers.

The *Marat/Sade* by Peter Weiss is based on the proposition that the inmates of the asylum of Charenton, under the direction of the Marquis de Sade, are to perform a play about the assassination of Marat by Charlotte Corday. The audience for this piece is the real audience in the theatre, who join forces with a number of French aristocrats invited to witness the spectacle.

Joan Littlewood's celebrated Theatre Workshop produced *Oh What a Lovely War!* in which a troupe of end-of-the-pier entertainers perform witty but pointed sketches and sing the songs of the First World War, thus telling the grimly familiar story with irony and a biting humour. More recently, Timberlake Wertenbaker's *Our Country's Good* centres on a production of Farquhar's play *The Recruiting Officer* given by a group of Australian convicts.

There's something essentially Brechtian about this concept in that it reminds the audience that they are watching a play by exploring and drawing attention to the conventions of theatre, the process of theatre and the possibilities of theatre. In the *Marat/Sade* we know perfectly well that we are watching actors pretending to be inmates of an asylum, pretending to be characters from the French revolution. Nevertheless, this very knowledge seems to give an added dimension to our experience. When the inmates rebel and run amok we enjoy being afraid even though we know that in reality there is nothing to be afraid of. We have been given an opportunity to savour fear in safe surroundings.

The same story can obviously be told in many different ways. What you are hoping to find is the most effective and powerful way of engaging the audience's attention.

The monologue or one-person play often appeals to the inexperienced playwright as it looks easier to deal with one character rather than several. But don't be deceived. The monologue is, in fact, an extraordinarily difficult form to master. If you do feel like trying it there are several guidelines which might help you to avoid the worst pitfalls. If only one character speaks then you will need to decide whether her audience is an unseen person (or people) or whether she is talking to herself (and, if so, why?). Or is she openly addressing the real audience as if they were watching her perform an act, or are the audience like peeping toms, observing, unobserved, witnesses to what is essentially a private ritual?

A monologue where the speaker simply gives an account of events which have already occurred won't be dramatic but if the audience can see events unfold before them it will. Does the monologue take your character on a journey? Or perhaps external circumstances change and she responds to those changes.

Although there is only one person in view in the monologue it is still possible to fill the stage with many characters, bringing to life people from your speaker's imagination or memory.

The monologue gives many opportunities for dramatic irony; the speaker may unwittingly condemn herself; the audience may instantly understand or gradually become aware of important facts in advance of the speaker.

Alan Bennett uses the dramatic potential of this form as a means of exploring the minutiae of apparently inconsequential lives with a gentle blend of humour and compassion. But never regard the monologue as a soft option for it demands a great deal of skill.

At the opposite end of the spectrum, the epic play, even if rarely financially feasible, is full of exciting and challenging possibilities.

If you get the opportunity to write for a large cast, whether in a community setting or elsewhere, jump at the chance and don't be afraid of the possible problems.

There's something immensely liberating about painting with bold strokes on a huge canvas, using large visual images — banners, giant puppets, massive artefacts — to stimulate the audience's imagination. It's sheer luxury to explore the possibilities of music and song with a cast of more than one hundred and an audience who may be promenading rather than sitting in neat rows. It's liberating but it can also be bewildering; the sheer logistics of scale make considerable demands on the writer. These plays need quite careful construction if they are not to sprawl, sag in the middle or simply meander.

David Edgar, in an article written for *The Guardian* about his experience of writing *Entertaining Strangers*, a community play for Dorchester, makes the distinction between large-scale plays and pageants. A pageant, he says, is "merely processional, lacking the dynamic of purpose" of a play. But he also believes that community or epic plays can and should have some of the elements of pageant, for example large self-contained units of action.

The real difference is that we must be able to identify with the main characters and to follow their stories with a strong sense of involvement to the climax.

Entertaining Strangers follows two main characters whose fortunes are eventually drawn together in a surprising but inevitable way during the cholera epidemic which struck the town in the 1860's.

All the characters are painted boldly but with clarity and care. They are idiosyncratic but not caricatured. Music, visual delights, set pieces which appeal to the imagination, evoking amazement, laughter, pure pleasure, surprise — all provide an unusually rich feast for eye and ear.

At the same time the economic and telling dialogue, pared down to its most vital essentials, communicates strongly and directly to the audience. The story moves forward all the time and the writer's intention is always very clear. The total experience is both moving and exhilarating, achieved as a result of a skilful blend of fine detail and bold effects.

Up to this point we have mostly thought in terms of a play which tells a linear story, with a definite beginning, middle and end. Yet it would be a pity if you were to confine yourself to work which is governed mostly by the laws of logic, ignoring the possibilities of writing plays which take effect more through the imagination than the intellect.

Just as you might dream the setting for your play, you might conceive of the entire piece of work in terms of a series of images and metaphors rather than a straightforward progression of ideas. It is possible to understand with the heart as well as with the intellect and a play that conveys your vision in this way can appeal directly to the audience on the same level as poetry or surreal art.

Seven Lears by Howard Barker is a complex and puzzling play, which gives fresh insight into the character of Shakespeare's Lear. Barker creates strong visual imagery: a red bird that later becomes a red monoplane, which the King in vain attempts to fly, and a group of mysterious ghost-like figures who haunt the King from boyhood, The play does not so much move forward as spread sideways; we gradually build up a picture of Lear as the character that Shakespeare created. We know that Lear will go mad, because we know Shakespeare's story, so our interest is in how this will happen and why.

The play affects the audience subliminally. At the interval there were few who were prepared to discuss or describe what had occurred on the stage. Afterwards I felt disturbed, puzzled, moved, intrigued. I needed time to sort out what I had seen and heard. Yet the images stayed with me, continuing to work in my imagination.

Perhaps you feel that you don't have the expertise to approach a piece of work in this way. It's mostly a question of trusting the power of your own imagination and the response of your audience. Although we are all capable of dreaming, whether awake or asleep, and of sensing a dimension beyond the everyday world, our opportunities to express and share these experiences are severely limited. A play which originates in your fantasies and dreams will naturally tap into the dreams of those who watch it.

Surreal theatre can utilise techniques more familiar to film or television — scenes may have no words but may be a collage of impressions; a stage is suddenly empty; a series of short, sharp scenes show different characters reacting to the same stimulus. It is not always necessary to explain.

Neither do you have to make rigid decisions about whether you are writing comedy or tragedy. Most stories have the potential for both within them and in the best plays they are not mutually exclusive. It's always a very powerful experience for the audience to laugh and then wish they hadn't or to cry when they have only just stopped laughing. Every comic situation has a tragic potential; even the most tragic situation can have a comic undertow.

At a recent workshop organised by the Welsh Theatre Writers' Union I asked the students to suggest simple stories which might be developed in a variety of ways. One student had read a snippet in a newspaper concerning an elderly couple who had seen a large hole developing in their house but had done nothing about it: the house eventually subsided.

This incident obviously has considerable dramatic potential and lends itself to several different approaches.

▷ The play could be developed along classic lines, using the first sighting of the hole as the trigger incident and working towards the climax, which might be the total subsidence of the house.

▷ The story could form the basis for a simple and tight two-hander, tracing the growing anxiety and trauma afflicting the elderly pair as circumstances moved further and further out of their control.

▷ The play could be a monologue, spoken by the old man or woman, or by their son, or even an official who hears of the case.

▷ It could be developed along epic lines, involving an entire street or town of characters, the men from the Ministry, hosts of builders, plumbers, reporters and bemused bystanders.

▷ It could be a surreal comedy in the style of Beckett, using a set which gradually subsides as the story progresses, till by the end only the heads of the characters are visible.

▷ It could expand to deal in depth with the wider environmental issues implicit in the subject, to explore the dwindling rights of the individual in an increasingly bureaucratic society. Or it could focus in sharply on the pain and bewilderment of one particular old lady who saw her home disappearing under a pile of rubble.

▷ Or the play could be a combination of all these things, taking something from all of the possible conventions to create a form which is distinctive and appropriate.

I feel that there are two broad approaches to the practical question of how to construct your play. I have already touched on both of them: the first

I would describe as 'schematic', the second as 'organic'. This is not to imply any criticism of one or the other. At certain points the first approach may feel more appropriate whilst in other circumstances you will tend towards the second.

In the 'schematic' approach you make a conscious and reasoned decision regarding structure and then you set about imposing that structure on your material.

For example, you may decide to use a time-slip device, employing flashbacks to penetrate the past life of a certain character. You now plot out scene by scene what will happen and where those flashbacks will occur. You make logical decisions about dramatic high points and about turning points in the story. You decide on the conclusion. All this should be done before beginning your first draft.

Or you may prefer the 'organic' approach. You have a few ideas about what you might like to see happen in your play but you aren't yet sure how or where these events will occur. You jot down these rather fluid thoughts without pre-empting what form they will eventually take. You know that there may be a scene involving A and B in which A verbally attacks B. You don't yet know what will spark this off or where it will occur. You feel that the play may move naturally towards a revelation by B about some event in the past but you don't yet know what that revelation is or how it will happen.

If this approach feels more comfortable for you, you may have to relinquish the security of knowing exactly where you are going in the first draft. Instead you will simply write and wait with interest to see how it turns out. This means that when the first draft is finished you will need to look at it quite dispassionately, almost as if it had been written by someone else. You will need to ask yourself a number of questions to determine how far instinct has taken you and what craft can now do to improve on the result. Above all, you will need to decide whether what you have written is sufficiently dramatic to capture the attention of the audience.

What is dramatic? Action is dramatic. The audience prefers to see events happen rather than hear a report. So a good maxim is: 'Show it, don't tell it.' Certainly don't do both: if you show something there is no need to tell about it too.

Change, development, movement within a character and in the relationship between characters is dramatic. So is conflict. Opposition of ideas, of temperaments, of aims, of ideals — all these produce conflict and so are dramatic. An unexpected turning point which leads events to shift is dramatic.

Self-questioning, moral dilemmas, difficult choices, a gap between what seems and what is — all these have the possibilities of drama in them.

Your story must keep moving forward, even if only by a series of very small steps. It must never be static. You must keep the audience wondering, longing to know what will happen next. And when it happens, they must feel certain that they always knew it would be so. This is Mamet's theory of 'inevitability'. Whilst events must seem newly-minted, surprising, amazing, unforeseen, they must also seem the obvious and unavoidable outcome of what has gone before.

Most plays, but by no means all plays, have a plot. The plot is the story, the sequence of events which you have imagined.

Perhaps you decide on one main story and one or several subsidiary stories, or sub-plots. The sub-plot (or plots) may be devised to echo or reflect on the main story or may have nothing at all to do with it. It may give some prominence to characters who are not important in the main plot, providing comic relief or ironic comment. You will still need to develop the sub-plot to a satisfactory conclusion: the audience will want to know what happened.

You often hear writers talking mysteriously about 'sub-text'. Sub-text is what characters are really thinking, wanting, intending, feeling, but not necessarily expressing. It is what lies beneath the surface of what they overtly say or do.

Your characters may be involved in private dramas or dilemmas, consumed with hidden desires, motivated by undisclosed ambitions, inhibited by secret fears. Occasionally these emotions will seep into the surface action but often they are left unstated and unresolved.

An awareness of this added dimension can bring subtlety and texture to your writing.

In the 'Made in Wales' workshops, I asked the students to answer two questions as they began to consider the construction of the first draft of their plays.

The first question is: "Why now?" and the second is: "Why here?"

Why should the play begin at this precise point and not at some other point in the story? To go back to the classical model: "What is the trigger incident?" Deciding on the point of entry to your story is a very important step. The attention of the audience must be quickly caught, their interest engaged, their excited anticipation assured.

Caryl Churchill's *Top Girls* begins with Isabella congratulating Marlene. The point of entry to the story is Marlene's appointment as managing director of the 'Top Girls' agency, though we do not learn this officially until the second act. It is this appointment which gives rise to the celebrity dinner party and which sets in motion the subsequent events.

The progression of events is not chronological; the last scene actually takes place a year before the others. In spite of the very odd structure it is amply justified. We have already made all our decisions about Marlene before we find out an integral and hitherto concealed fact. Angie, who appears unexpectedly and incongruously in Marlene's glossy office early in Act Two, is in fact her daughter.

The beginning of your play is crucial. This is where you capture your audience or lose them. Unless they are quickly asking "What's going to happen?" or "How can that be?", they will not make the necessary commitment of energy and imagination to stay with it.

It's a good idea to plunge straight into the action without too much preamble. Establishing what has already happened, explanations as to why people are where they are, long-drawn-out accounts of previous circumstances and events are all tedious and unnecessary. Imagine, instead, that the audience opens a door and your characters are there, half-way through a sentence, already deeply engaged in discussion, argument, or dilemma. This must seem to be the very point at which the action begins to move forward irresistibly, taking the audience with it. The excitement and danger of theatre is being aware that you are on a journey with no idea of the destination. The playwright's job is to try to overcome the audience's natural tendency to want to jump off the train.

The arrival of strangers or unexpected guests is a common device for triggering off the action. Think of Blanche Dubois in Tennessee Williams' *A Streetcar Named Desire*, Goldberg and McCann in Pinter's *The Birthday Party* or Black Jack Musgrave in Arden's *Serjeant Musgrave's Dance*. They serve to spark off a chain of events or bring about sudden changes in a family or community. But the newcomer only acts as a catalyst, carrying the match to light the fire already laid. This is why events, though surprising, must also feel inevitable. We should sense that the dice was already loaded; all that was needed was the introduction of one more factor and the game would be under way.

With the question: "Why here?" it is important to find a setting that will be revealing, with the maximum scope for exploring your ideas.

Be adventurous in your choice of setting; reject your first idea and search for something more pertinent. Plays set in a suburban semi have to work twice as hard to be startling, original, thought-provoking or even simply interesting. Of course, you could make the very mundaneness of the setting work to your advantage. Ayckbourn has proved that the most familiar settings can inform and energise an idea. Whether he divides the set to give us a view of two different households simultaneously, or shows us the same household assembled in the same place but at different times, he is using the audience's recognition of themselves to hook them into what he has to say.

If his settings were not so painfully familiar, his critique of middle-class mores would not hit home so effectively. We see; we recognise; we wince with recognition; but still we are incapable of resisting his appeal.

Sometimes the setting is obviously dictated by the demands of the story.

Brian Clark's *Whose Life is it Anyway?* deals with the dilemmas of a man severely injured in a road accident. The hospital setting, with all its sterile medical paraphernalia, underpins the central question of the play: should a man be kept alive against his will or should he be allowed to choose his own death?

Peter Nichols uses the hospital setting more symbolically in *The National Health*, where the dreary and run-down public ward becomes a potent metaphor for a nation in decline.

The action of Stephen Lowe's vivid adaptation of *The Ragged-Trousered Philanthropists* takes place mostly 'on site', as the characters feverishly paint and decorate a house in full view of the audience. We are able to identify strongly with the trials of the underpaid worker and the strong political message of the piece as we watch men clamber up and down ladders.

Trafford Tanzi by Clare Luckham is set in a wrestling ring, where Tanzi, the central character, symbolically plays out the various battles of her life as a woman. The audience in the theatre find themselves 'playing' the audience at these bouts, quickly developing a partisan interest in their outcome.

My play *Free 'n' Lovely* looks at some of the same issues in the setting of a seedy beauty contest. Joe, the compere, assaults the real audience with his sexist jokes and distasteful commentary on events. The real audience find themselves actively engaged in making decisions affecting the outcome of the contest; they are asked to cast votes for winners of individual rounds and to express their preference for tights and stockings. In production this device worked rather well. During the interval at one show, I overheard two young girls arguing over which contestant was going to win. "She won't . . . she's too old," said one, "And anyway, her legs are too thin."

Stephen Jeffreys' play *Valued Friends* is about the relationship between a group of friends sharing a London flat and the changes which occur when they find themselves part of the property boom. As money enters their lives and begins to take its inevitable toll, so the setting evolves to reflect the progress of the action. The shabby student pad with its radical posters is steadily transformed into a sleek and sterile black and white environment where friendship is strained to the hilt amidst the expensively tubular furniture. The setting silently and unequivocally tells the story as effectively as the dialogue.

The poet Adrienne Rich remarked that women live their lives in one room. 'One room' plays do seem particularly female in form, the action blossoming untidily in a single multi-purpose setting which reflects the sometimes chaotic but creative nature of the characters' lives. Such settings make no distinction between places to work and places to play, between private and public, between inner and outer, between past and present.

Pat Lewis's workshop play *Iron them Dry* was just such a piece. It contained and described her whole childhood. The objects in it became potent symbols of her struggle to emerge from that lively, warm but restrictive environment: the orange divided into segments which the children in the street stole from her; her father's possessions she was never allowed to touch; her mother's hated apron; the table covered with newspaper.

Such a play will need a strong central character to draw the audience through the action. If the audience can identify with your protagonist then her world will, for the space of the play, become their world.

Endings are as important as beginnings but they usually cause problems, even for an experienced writer. It is obviously desirable that the ending should work either by resolving the puzzle you have presented or by posing more questions for the audience to take away with them. An unsatisfactory ending can easily obliterate all that precedes it, leaving the audience feeling mystified, frustrated or cheated. Again, it may be helpful to look back at Mamet's statement. Does the ending feel inevitable or is it contrived, a pat solution to the problems you have raised? Sometimes you have a good idea of how you want your play to end and can work systematically towards that resolution. But there are instances where the ending surprises you as much as it will surprise the audience. Then it seems more a question of going into reverse and looking for ways to lay clues for the audience.

'Signalling' is an important device; it is a way of giving the audience an opportunity to predict the outcome without actually pre-empting it. When it happens they can feel satisfied that they saw it coming without losing the thrill of surprise.

In *Top Girls* Churchill signals the row between Marlene and her sister that will occur in the final scene with a single exchange in the very first scene:

ISABELLA Do you have a sister?
MARLENE Yes, in fact.

The 'in fact' is deliberately awkward and seems to indicate an unspoken problem. There is then another brief exchange which gives a hint of an aspect of Marlene yet to be revealed:

NIJO   Haven't you ever felt like that? You've all felt/like that.
ISABELLA You thought that your life was over but it wasn't.
MARLENE Yes but only for a few hours, not twenty years.

Sometimes a play can work well emotionally even though it may have little or no discernible structure. Endesha Ida Mae Holland's *From the Mississippi Delta* is basically a large chunk of autobiography. The writer draws on various traditions, using song, story-telling and vigorous physical movement to paint a colourful picture of life in the American South. It seems to grow organically, building up gradually into a collage of incidents and people. The first act is richer in incident than the second, which rather tails away. But in the theatre, in Annie Castledine's stunning production, the play worked because the story is so passionate, so truthful, so vivid and so important.

Just as there are performances that are technically perfect but emotionally sterile so there are plays which are perfectly constructed but which fail to generate any warmth or genuine response in the audience. That's why it's good to remember that some plays can get away with breaking every rule in the book. If they make your hair stand on end with sheer excitement, make you laugh or cry (or, better still, laugh *and* cry), then they have proved themselves.

Perhaps what I am saying is this: don't become too obsessed with structure. Concentrate instead on what you want to say and focus on discovering the truth of it.

I have discussed two radically different approaches — the 'schematic' and the 'organic' — and one of them will probably appeal to you more than the other.

You may feel you need the security of a tight and organised framework from which to work. This is fine, provided you are prepared to throw it all up in the air, give in to sudden impulse and to accept that you are not working in a medium where logic will or should always prevail.

If you feel you need to tell your story quickly and passionately, even chaotically, that too is fine as long as you are prepared to look at what you've written as a blueprint and to ask yourself some searching and critical questions about how it will work for an audience.

The form you do choose eventually may not be the form you originally thought of but the process of discovery should free your imagination and let you communicate in the most effective way possible.

Project: Developing a story

FIND A STORY THAT APPEALS TO YOU IN A NEWSPAPER

▷ Think about how the story could be told in dramatic form and then:
  a) Plot the story as an epic play with a huge cast. Think in terms of visual effects, music, pageantry, set pieces, etc.
  b) Develop the story through visual images, poetry and ritual.
  c) Create a central character and write a monologue in which she/he reveals an unexpected involvement in the events described.
  d) Produce a detailed scenario, giving a scene-by-scene breakdown of what will happen.
  e) Highlight the changes and shifts that serve to propel the action forward.

▷ 'Cloudburst': Jot down at random all the ideas you have about the story. Look for possible connections between the scenes.

CHAPTER SIX

Into the First Draft

– Finding a title – Stage directions –
– Introducing the characters – Layout and presentation –
– Beginning – Writer's block – Getting back to basics –
– Re-inventing the characters – Putting pen to paper –

It's time to start work on your first draft. In the workshops I insisted on using this term because I wanted to emphasise the difference between work you do for yourself and work you intend to show to others.

I regard the first draft of a play as a very rough outline, the equivalent of the artist's first sketch for a painting. It is the solving of a puzzle, a journey undertaken alone. It is private work, for your eyes only.

The first draft is your best means of testing out your ideas in a safe setting. It is where you can make mistakes, experiment with several different ways of doing the same thing, disappear down blind alleys.

The first drafts of all my recent plays are written in pencil. They are practically illegible. But, when I first started to write, the first draft had a much neater appearance, as if I expected to be able to organise my thoughts and express them with clarity at the first attempt. Now I accept that it will always take two (and usually three) complete versions of a text before it feels ready to show to anyone at all.

The British Museum houses many manuscripts of works later to be famous. It's strangely encouraging to look at a page of scribbled text, riddled with crossings-out, peppered with second thoughts and indecipherable notes, and to know that the work is now published, recognised and acclaimed. In case you can't travel to look at these texts I'll offer you, as an example, page 1 of the very first draft of my play *Self Portrait*. (There were three drafts and numerous subsequent cuts and revisions.) You'll see that I've paid little attention to layout and even less to legibility. All that can come later. It's full of coded messages to myself, which I may or may not decipher at a later stage. I'm obviously confident that no one needs to be able to read it but me.

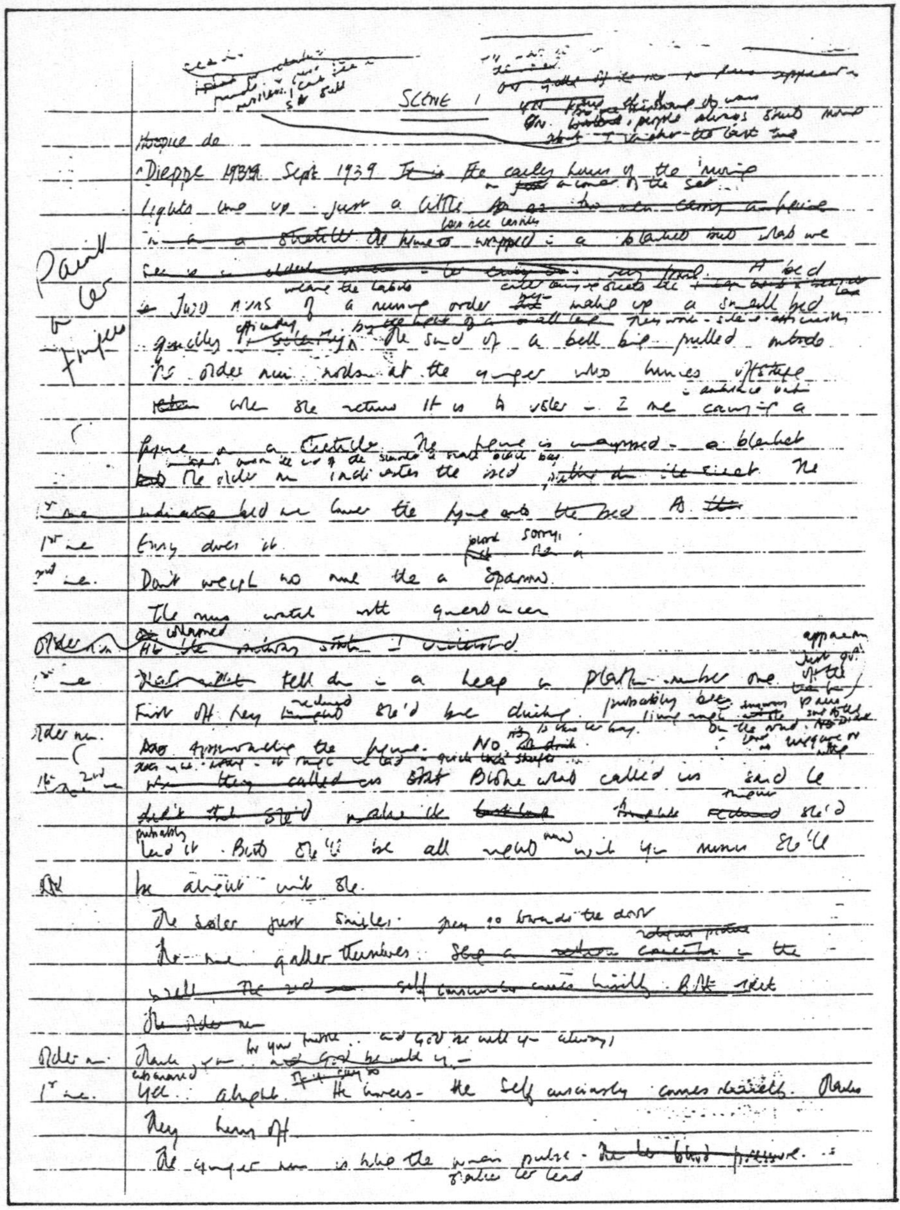

The first draft: page 1

Writing the first draft is both exhilarating and terrifying. Will you write with great abandon for twenty pages and then run out of steam? Will the characters you have imagined spring readily to life or will they die on you? Will the story develop along the lines you have envisaged or will it twist and turn down unexpected routes?

One way or another, you had better prepare yourself for a long siege. Take the telephone off the hook, tell your friends you're busy, invite no one, accept no invitations. Organise some food that's easy to grab, wrap up warm (even in summer your body temperature will mysteriously plummet while you're writing), close the door, sit down and . . . think of a title.

Strictly speaking, you don't actually need a title at this stage. But it does help to focus the mind on the job in hand. Finding a title has two main functions: it encourages you to concentrate your attention on what you *think* you are writing about and it will persuade you that you are actually about to begin work. A title at the top of the page is a very convincing statement of intent.

It also means that, when people ask you what you are working on, you can simply reply: "It's called: *Bolt from the Blue* or *Tulips* or *Going Nowhere.*" This sounds purposeful and gives you an excuse not to tell the whole story. At this stage in the proceedings you will need to go underground about what you intend to write. The more you describe it, talk about it or analyse it, the less reason there will be to write.

Writing should be a compulsion. You write because you must, because you need to express what you feel, to communicate what you see. If you have already expressed it, that need will be dissipated, the urgency will be diffused, and it will prove that much harder to write anything at all.

Titles are like a banner proclaiming your intention, first to yourself, but eventually to your audience.

The title *Self Portrait* suggests several things, all of which should provoke some interest. It could be:

1. A play about an artist.
2. A play about an artist painting a self portrait or an artist who often painted self portraits.
3. A play about an artist whose portraits of others were also in some way self portraits.
4. A play about the writer herself, about biography, about understanding oneself, about images of women.
5. Or any combination of these.

My play *Dancing in the Dark* is about Blanche, an elderly woman in an old people's home. The title:

1.   Evokes the song of the same name, fashionable when Blanche was a younger woman, and so stirring memories of her past.
2.   Uses 'dancing' metaphorically, ie 'celebrating'. It is a counter-balance to life 'in the dark', ie when everything seems gloomy or hopeless.
3.   Alludes to sequences in the play where dancing is an important motif.

A title should suggest the various levels on which your play is to function, thus drawing the audience into your world.

To begin with everything is extremely fluid. You may start off with one title and end up with another. The first title might simply be your working title, one that you use until you have discovered your real subject. My play *Geraniums* started life as *The Fourth of October*. This referred to the date in 1936 on which the events described in the play occurred. *Geraniums* surfaced as a title at draft three and is a reference to a recurring motif in the text.

There are geraniums in the window box in the narrow East End street. The plants are lovingly tended, somehow surviving in spite of the dirt and dust. Later they are perceived as a symbol of survival itself. Indeed, when Zelda, a woman we see both as her young self and also as an elderly woman, paints a picture, the subject is . . . geraniums.

One-word titles can be succinct and powerful. *Bent* by Martin Sherman is about two homosexuals in a concentration camp. *Good* by C.P. Taylor is also about the Nazi regime. The title has a deadly irony: Halder, a 'good' man, a liberal man, is slowly and apparently innocently drawn into serving the Nazis. Barrie Keeffe's *Gotcha* gives a sharp foretaste of his tight exploration of disenchanted and inarticulate youth.

You can plunder the *Oxford Dictionary of Quotations* for a title or draw on your knowledge of poetry, the Bible or Shakespeare.

A title should give a hint of what the play will say and a flavour of how it will be said. We can guess that Joe Orton's *What the Butler Saw* is intended to be provocative, as is Chris Wilkinson's *Plays for Rubber Go-Go Girls*.

A title can intrigue, like Stoppard's *Rosencrantz and Guildenstern are Dead* and *Every Good Boy Deserves Favour*. The latter makes use of the child's mnemonic to draw us into the world of music. The play incorporates a full orchestra, but the title also hints, in its quaintly Victorian idiom, at systems of praise and blame in a repressive society.

Once you have found a title you will undoubtedly begin to worry about stage directions and layout. Even though it isn't really necessary to clarify this until you reach your second draft I know how much problems with the mechanics of writing can impede and inhibit a beginner.

Stage directions are simply clues to the director. They can't take the place of dialogue, nor can they be used to explain whatever dialogue has failed to clarify. Only write down what is necessary, illuminating and helpful.

The action of your play will spring from the dialogue and the interplay of characters. The position of a piece of furniture may be essential to the plot and the fact that an actor moves to the left rather than the right may be crucial, but neither can compensate for gaps in the action.

As a rule of thumb it's preferable to keep stage directions to the bare minimum. But they can contain vital information. For example, in *Dancing in the Dark* :

PAUL LOOKS AT HIS WATCH. SOMETHING HE OFTEN DOES.

And later in the same scene . . .

BLANCHE   (THROWING HIM OFF) Silly? Who you calling silly?
          SHE BELTS HIM ACROSS THE FACE.

And then . . .

PAUL   I didn't WANT to use force but . . .
          HE GRABS HOLD OF HER. SHE STRUGGLES. HE
          RESTRAINS HER ONLY WITH CONSIDERABLE
          DIFFICULTY.

Here the stage directions obviously form part of the action and are used to complement the dialogue. The actors' interpretation of them will add to their understanding of how the scene is to be played. Yet it is already obvious from the dialogue that tempers are frayed and patience is running thin; the directions simply add to that impression.

If the arrangement of furniture, the colour of curtains, the position of doors or windows, etc. is integral, either to the plot or to the visual metaphor you are creating, then you must obviously indicate as much in your directions. Similarly, if, in the course of the action, it is crucial that a character moves, then you must specify. The plotting of moves is otherwise the job of the director.

In any event, if your play goes into production, the design can only evoke what you describe. It is almost always impossible for what you visualise to be replicated detail for detail.

Sometimes new playwrights will preface the text with lengthy descriptions of each character. Not only do these cover details of dress and personal appearance, they also frequently include indications of personality traits, habits and behaviour. Overwritten descriptions are not only unnecessary, they also show up a writer's lack of confidence. A basic list of characters is all you need, with their approximate ages, an indication of a job or occupation, and reference to the relationship between them if relevant. For example:

JANE SMITH   :   a novelist, mid-40's
NIGEL SMITH   :   her son, a student, early 20's
EMMA BROWN :   a dancer, about 19, NIGEL'S fiancée

On the first appearance of a character it may be helpful to give a few brief notes regarding anything of particular signficance in appearance or manner.

This is how I introduce PAUL and BLANCHE on page 1 of *Dancing in the Dark* :

> PAUL IS A MAN IN HIS EARLY 30'S, SHARPLY DRESSED FOR HIGH-POWERED WORK IN THE CITY. HE SEEMS UNDER CONSIDERABLE STRESS. HE CARRIES A SMALL HOLDALL AND AN EMPTY BIRDCAGE. BLANCHE IS A WOMAN IN HER 70'S. SHE DOES NOT APPEAR FRAIL, THOUGH SHE LIMPS SLIGHTLY. SHE LOOKS ROSY AND ROBUST, A COUNTRY WOMAN. SHE WEARS AN OLD BUT SERVICEABLE COAT, AND A SMALL HAT, AND CARRIES A GOOD, IF BATTERED, HANDBAG.

Later I introduce JOHN BUDGEN:

> HE IS A SOLID, MILD AND SOMEWHAT WEARY MAN, PROBABLY ABOUT 40. HE WEARS A SHORT WHITE COAT OVER BAGGY TROUSERS AND A HAND-KNITTED PULLOVER. HE CARRIES A LARGE BUNCH OF KEYS.

These descriptions would give both director and actors important information about the first impression these characters should give to the audience. The clothes carry obvious messages. In the case of Paul and Budgen they indicate profession and self-image. In the case of Blanche they indicate her background and age and convey a sense that this is some sort of special occasion.

Most actors resent being told by the writer exactly how to deliver lines: the sense should lie within the text itself. Just occasionally it will help to use pointers to stress how a line should be spoken, e.g. (SARCASTICALLY) "I hope you have a good time." Or (SCREAMING) "Go away!"

The important thing about layout and presentation, as with the text itself, is to aim for maximum clarity, minimum confusion. Distinguish clearly between dialogue and stage directions and make sure that the names of characters are ranged to the left, well separated from the main text.

If you are typing your first draft, or using a word processor, you may as well lay your work out correctly from the start. There's no need for red type, underlining or other decorative touches. Simply use capitals for anything which isn't actually spoken, keeping the dialogue itself in lower case. Always use double line spacing as it makes for much easier reading.

Writing isn't simply a question of putting words on paper. The subterranean process is at work even when you're doing something quite different. It ticks away beneath the surface; ideas cross-fertilise, germinate, begin to grow, all without your conscious intervention. One day you will sit for hours gazing out of the window and writing nothing. The next day you will sit down and the words will pour out. Mostly it's hard work, but just occasionally you feel a sense of such rightness, such elation, that all the hours of pencil-biting frustration are forgotten.

Learning to write enough to bring a piece of work to fruition requires self-discipline. It will certainly mean sitting down at your desk when you don't feel like it at all. It will mean staying there when the words just don't come, or when they're the wrong words, or awkward words, disturbing words.

Beginning is always the worst part. You need to summon up great reserves of courage, to draw on huge resources of energy, both physical and mental. It's tiring work, lonely work: there won't be too many office parties. Coming to terms with the isolation and the frustration are all part of the process.

I usually begin with a strange mixture of excitement and terror. I am desperate to start writing. The play is boiling up in my brain. But still I defer the moment when I'll actually pick up pencil and paper and begin. All writers have their private rituals: sharpening all the pencils, setting out rubber, ruler, etc. at a particular angle, walking round the block in a clockwise direction on Mondays, Wednesdays and Fridays and anti-clockwise on Tuesdays and Thursdays, making endless cups of tea. All are essentially displacement activities designed to defer the moment when there will be no option but to start.

Some writers can only work if they set themselves a deadline, aiming to complete a certain stage of the work by a given date. It induces a sense of pressure which may be stimulating but the feeling of failure and depression that occurs if you miss a deadline can be counter-productive. If this is your first play then you can have no realistic idea of how long it will take you to write it until you try.

There are certain problems which every writer experiences, whether it is their first or thirty-first play. Perhaps the most difficult aspect of being a writer is the sense of total isolation and the extreme vulnerability this produces. The knowledge that the difficulties you are experiencing are not unique may help you through barren patches and persuade you not to give up completely.

One familiar problem is a loss of impetus, a flagging in energy after the first few days. You set off in high spirits, full of inspiration, and quite sure you know what you're doing. For a while all goes amazingly well. You write a lot; you feel in touch with your characters, excited by your story. Then suddenly — full stop. The characters seem to have died on you; the story feels empty and pointless.

I've already compared the process of writing a play to falling in love. Let's return to the analogy. You start off by gently flirting with the idea. It attracts you, but it's nothing serious. Gradually the feeling builds in intensity. Sitting down to begin the first draft is where you finally stop trying to escape, where you drop your defences and realise the inevitability of it all. Such intensity, so much accumulated emotion, so many plans, dreams, hopes. You plunge in, regardless of danger. And, for a while, the sheer momentum of your own passion carries you forward. The excitement is unbearable. You can't eat, you can't sleep. Nothing in the world exists except this.

Then, sadly perhaps, reality begins to impinge. Dreaming of being a writer is one thing. Actually writing, day in, day out, confronting the matter-of-factness of it, is quite another. Inspiration, like passion, may fade, but less glamorous attributes such as dogged perseverance and determination can help you to keep going through sticky patches.

If you are stuck, how can you get unstuck?

Sometimes it's simply a question of brain fatigue or even physical exhaustion. Never underestimate the sheer hard work involved in writing. You are concentrating hard, possibly sitting in an unaccustomed position, for hours on end. Small wonder that back injuries are the typical industrial injury for writers, as are stiff necks and aching eyes. So, if you are stuck, perhaps you are tired and need a break. A day spent walking in the country or by the sea, or doing something ordinary like wandering round the shops, gardening or cooking can be revitalising. You aren't a machine and the body can't function well under pressure for too long. Sometimes a day or two spent away from writing can help you to get started again, refreshed, relaxed, and with a new lease of energy.

Never make the mistake of regarding writing as something mechanical. You are delving into very deep places, tapping into areas usually left unexplored. So you must be prepared for pain, for confrontation, for self-doubt. Writing will put you in touch with your own feelings and with the world around you in a totally unexpected and unavoidable way. There will undoubtedly be times when you'll wish you'd left well alone; you will experience days of appalling despair, but also moments of pure ecstasy. And, yes, there *is* such a thing as writer's block. Sometimes you sit in front of the blank page for days and not a single useful thought comes into your head.

You decide to leave it till tomorrow. Tomorrow is the same, only worse. You begin to panic, to question the basic premise of your play. You look at what you've already written and it seems totally useless. Anyway, what's the point of inventing characters and making up things for them to say? Sudden and inexplicable loss of confidence is hard to overcome, even for a very experienced writer. I can only suggest methods I've sometimes found effective.

Sit down quietly and consider why you thought it so important to write this play in the first place. Try to get back in touch with the passion which originally motivated you. Challenge yourself on the original premise. Perhaps there's something basically wrong or perhaps you don't really believe in what you're saying.

If you can possibly start writing again, do, even if it's only a quarter of a page and even if it looks like rubbish. It may not be. As with any undertaking which requires a great deal of self-motivation, the sheer act of doing it, however badly, is strangely endorsing and sometimes leads to a renewal of confidence.

Self-discipline is crucial to a writer but you have to learn to strike the balance between being too hard on yourself and being too soft. Too hard is being inflexible — setting a very rigid timetable and then being furious with yourself when you fail to adhere to it. Too soft is using any excuse not to sit down to write. The middle way is to listen to your own internal rhythms, to try to work with them, not against them. Some days are good days; some days are bad days. Be compassionate to yourself but don't lose sight of your aim. Strong motivation and a clear sense of purpose will help you survive the worst days.

Sometimes you temporarily lose your way. You want to write but you don't know what to write next. Everything goes out of focus and you start to thrash about looking for clues. When this happens, sit down and write yourself a statement of intent:

"This is a play about . . . " Or even: "I *think* this is a play about . . . "

Again, you are trying to get back in touch with your original impetus. If it helps to look afresh at your research, or to re-read a book or revisit a place which first excited you, then do that.

Writers who don't have a great deal of experience of writing plays sometimes complain that characters are getting out of hand. This is actually a good rather than a bad sign, though it can be baffling at first. Characters who began by existing only in your imagination, and so were completely under your control, slowly come to life and acquire a mysterious will of their own. Learn to listen to what they say; be prepared to give in to their demands.

I remember driving down the motorway from Devon to Bristol after several days spent wrestling with *Self Portrait*. I was feeling exhausted. Then Gwen John started to speak to me. Her voice (as in real life) was quiet, but extremely persuasive. I tried to ignore it but she insisted on being heard. I drew into the next service area and wrote down verbatim everything she said. At that point I had no idea of how I could use her words but I felt instinctively that I couldn't ignore them. In fact, I was to change the course of the action to give her monologue prominence at the end of Act One, even though both the intensity and the content surprised me as much as anyone. In performance I found the audience particularly responsive to that speech which, by some quite mysterious process, evidently expressed the very essence of the character.

Sometimes you find yourself struggling with the number of characters you have created. Perhaps, even early on, it becomes apparent that two characters are serving virtually the same function in the plot. You find it hard to differentiate between them or to give each a sufficiently substantial role to play. You could make a rapid decision to jettison one before you get too attached to him or you could persevere to the end of the first draft, making a note to yourself to pay special attention to his function when you begin to consider the second.

If you have decided to adopt a schematic approach to your play you will have worked out exactly what will happen from start to finish, scene by scene. But what if you get as far as Scene 7 and suddenly feel that you've omitted something quite crucial? What can you do? It's probably a mistake to go back to the beginning and start again. Better to keep going, making a note to yourself of the omission and some ideas about how it might be dealt with. Perhaps, in the second draft, you will be able to insert a scene (or several scenes) to explore what has been left out or understated. Or it may be possible to insert new speeches into existing scenes. If you suddenly become aware that you have left a whole aspect of the subject unexplored your task will be a little more tricky, possibly involving skilful weaving of new material through the entire text. The important thing is not to panic but to keep going to the end of the first draft.

If you are working in a more organic way, without concrete plans or a definite outline of scenes, you may be prone to a sudden loss of focus. When using this method it's probably advisable to try to complete your first draft in as short a time as possible, relying on the sheer momentum of your imaginative process to propel you forward. You can organise, tidy, rationalise afterwards. Your primary aim at this stage is to get something down on paper before it disappears into thin air. It's frightening to lose the thread when working in this way but speed and intense concentration will operate in your favour.

It's perfectly natural to feel insecure about starting to write. You know by now that it's a big undertaking. Reassure yourself that you have done the necessary groundwork, that your research is complete, that you have no further questions about layout and techniques.

You have been preparing to write a play, dreaming about it, thinking about it. Now you must make a serious commitment of time and energy.

Make up your mind not to allow anything to distract you or to persuade you off-course. Be determined to keep going till you have some sort of finished piece.

Forget all the brilliant plays you have seen or read. This is *your* play and it will exist in its own right. This is a time of high excitement, of great tension, of fear and anticipation. There are moments of sheer panic and days of total desperation. And at the end of it all . . . exhaustion, relief, total disbelief, and an extraordinary sense of achievement. Your first draft . . . rough, imperfect, full of glaring gaps and inconsistencies, but there on the page, existing in its own right . . . finished.

CHAPTER SEVEN

Shaping the First Draft

– Re-reading the text – Becoming objective –
– The 'story-board' – Assessing the pace –
– Beginnings and endings – Analysing the characters –
– Who's talking? – Balancing the speeches –
– Radical solutions – Focus and clarity –
– The fat draft – The thin draft – The tight draft –
– Discovering the sub-text – Being your own judge –

"Dear Sheila,

Here is my 'almost' first draft — 'almost' in the sense of it not being all that long rather than anything else. There are, of course, lots of things that I know need to be worked on and changed etc. There are also many things I've overlooked. These are a few things I would like to say:

1. I have found length or the lack of it a problem.
2. I want to write more 'songs' for it: in particular I want to research and use a 'ballad' working song in Act Two. There are several scenes I still want to write . . ."

"Dear Sheila,

Finished! Never thought I'd actually get there. Do you think the ending is too tame? I did have another ending, but that seemed a little melodramatic to me. Look forward to hearing your comments."

These letters from two of the women in the 'Made in Wales' Workshops capture perfectly the mixture of euphoria and uncertainty which characterises this stage in the process of writing a play.

It's a great relief to have written something — anything — and to have 'finished' it; to have told the story, solved the puzzle. But almost immediately you begin to realise that this isn't the end, rather the beginning of a long and often arduous process of honing, revising and refining.

The workshop participants were in the unusual position of having an external critic to read their first drafts. Unless you are a member of such a group you will have to learn to be your own critic. Before you can do that, however, you need to distance yourself. It's not a good idea to try to begin work on a second draft immediately; you will need a cooling-off period.

Your first draft was probably written in white heat. Writing it plunged you into an enchanted world of your own creation. You have heard voices; you have been other people. You have been carried along on the tide of your imagination, discovering in yourself an amazing fund of energy and an extraordinary will to continue, against all odds. It has been an intoxicating, terrifying and unique experience.

Now, without losing too much of that excitement or sheer energy, you must try to look at what you've written with a more dispassionate eye. You must now employ a more conscious craft to make the text as clear, as focussed and as accessible as possible.

The first draft tells you what it is you want to communicate. The second draft attempts to discover the most effective means of communicating it.

When you feel ready, read the text through. Give yourself plenty of time and read it without stopping. You are trying to gain a very general impression of what is there. What you find may surprise you; it may even shock you. The gap between what you intended to write, or what you thought you were writing, and what is actually on the page may alarm you. But don't be too despondent or judgemental. Accept the play at its face value and ask yourself some simple questions.

Does it work? Does it have cohesion, make sense either in literal or metaphorical terms? Is it interesting or boring? Are you, the reader, propelled along from page to page by a desire to know what will happen next?

If it seems a million miles away from what you had originally intended, ask yourself how and why this has happened. Is the gap a sign of a development of the original idea or an inability to realise what you had set out to do? Can you be happy, in broad terms, with what you have actually written or do you feel as if you have diverged too much from your primary aim?

Don't be too hasty to reject what is there on the page. It has its own validity. What you thought you could write and what you are now reading may indeed be two different things but it's a mistake to assume that the deviation necessarily implies failure.

Although you will clearly still feel passionately identified with what you have written, by now a degree of objectivity will be creeping in. You will begin to have a sense of the play as an entity, separate from you, its creator.

To help with this process it might be useful to make a 'story-board', which is a cartoon-style frame-by-frame representation of each development in the story. Underneath each frame describe briefly what happens.

Looking at the matchstick men and the accompanying captions can have a curiously calming effect. The 'story-board' (a device borrowed from the world of film-making) should help you to spot any glaring inconsistencies in the plot, any obvious hiatuses, or unexplained and awkward leaps in the action.

1. Jane and Brian argue.   2. Fred comes in.   3. Jane accuses Brian. Fred runs off.

A 'story-board' can reveal an obvious gap where a new scene is needed or it can show that you have repeated a scene.

This could lead you to a more detailed examination of the structure. The basic question you must ask yourself is: is it dramatic?

What develops, scene by scene, from start to finish? A scene in which nothing changes is one which, in theatrical terms, does nothing to move the action forward. Are there scenes which are essentially static? If so, could they be dispensed with or rewritten so as to incorporate more action?

Perhaps your play feels too episodic? Have you written a series of short, undeveloped incidents, impressions rather than satisfying scenes? Could you expand these episodes, giving them more depth, subtlety and scope? Or should some of them be combined to make one scene? Look closely to see what happens in each episode and see whether they are still strictly necessary to the action.

What about pace? Does the action move too slowly, dragging its feet? Do you repeat yourself, telling the audience the same thing in many different ways?

To vary pace, look for the possibility of introducing turning points —
moments in the story when events make a sudden shift in a new direction,
stimulating new interest, arousing new curiousity. Turning points will
break up the steady flow of the action, thus preventing tedium. They
aren't necessarily twists in the plot but may arise quite naturally from
what has gone before. Up to that point, events seem to be running in one
direction; after that point, they develop along different lines.

Does the story make sense, either in logical or metaphorical terms?
Given the situation you have set up, and the characters you have created,
does the story seem to move inexorably towards its climax? Is there any
possibility of signalling that climax along the way?

Is the climax well-realised, bringing together all the elements of the
play, or are there too many loose ends, unresolved plot lines, sub-plots
lost along the way, characters who have faded from view?

Look closely at the beginning of your play. It is perfectly natural for the
first few scenes to show signs of uncertainty but you may now find
elements that are plainly inconsistent with what subsequently develops.
This is easy enough to remedy in the second draft when you can retrace
your steps and put up the appropriate signposts.

Does the opening scene lead rapidly into the play, immediately exciting
interest, raising all sorts of questions, establishing intriguing situations?
Will it make the audience long to know what will happen next? Is there a
feeling that, given all the elements of the situation, something must
happen? Or is the beginning a tedious preamble, a long drawn-out
'setting-up', which will make us feel like screaming: "Get on with the
story!"

Now look at the end. Is it a satisfying resolution to what has gone
before? It isn't necessarily desirable to resolve all the questions. Indeed,
your overt intention could be to send the audience out with a great deal
to think about and with many questions still whirling around in their
minds. But even in this case your ending should seem to be the most
likely outcome of what you have explored and developed throughout the
play; it should satisfy either in logical or imaginative terms.

Sometimes a first draft doesn't have a real ending: it just fizzles out.
Look at the last few scenes of your play. Do they show signs of exhaustion
or a desire to finish the thing off as quickly as possible? Now is your
opportunity to go back to those scenes and, with renewed energy, to see
if they can be improved or developed.

Endings are always a problem. I think it's because they feel so definitive:
your last word on the subject. There's nothing wrong with keeping your
options open for the moment, with an alternative ending up your sleeve
until you are more sure of the shape of the whole piece.

Now look at the characters you have created. Are they clearly differentiated? Does each have a distinct and special role to play?

Is there sufficient conflict within characters and between characters? Does that conflict seem to be inevitable, arising naturally from the situations and juxtapositions you have set up or is it artificial, giving a sense of having been grafted on for effect?

If you have any doubts about your characters it might be useful to tell the story from the point of view of each character in turn. (In plays with a large cast just select the main characters.) You can approach this as a very matter-of-fact exercise. Write the character's name, eg BLANCHE (from my play *Dancing in the Dark*). Then write a speech giving a breakdown of the events she experiences in the course of the play:

"My son Paul brought me here in his car. It turned out to be an old people's home. I hated it. They treated me like a child. But I had these extraordinary dreams. I kept thinking of other places, other people. They sent me this girl Lisa; she was doing community service. She was a poor scrap, but we got on alright. I made her laugh. In the end she took me out of the home in my wheelchair. She was like a different person, full of beans. She put me under a tree while she danced. (I died)".

If you find that you can't do this satisfactorily it probably means that the character's role is insufficiently developed. Perhaps you can only do it up to a certain point of the play or for certain scenes. Does this mean that the character disappears altogether or for long periods?

When you have told the story from the point of view of each character ask yourself whether anyone is redundant. Or maybe two characters are so similar in role and function that they could easily be merged into a single, more satisfactory, individual. It's never easy to throw a character overboard — it feels a little like killing off an old friend — but sometimes it's a decision which has to be taken in the interests of focus and economy.

Remember too that your characters will be brought to life by actors who will want to know their own character's motivation. If a character is underdeveloped, or if she has no easily discernible 'line', then it will be impossible for the actor to make her live and breathe for the audience. It's better to lose a flimsy character (and to concentrate on developing those that remain) than to continue working with one who is not fully realised.

Look closely at the dialogue. Experiment by covering up the names in the margin. Is it easy to tell who is talking? If it isn't it may mean that all the characters sound alike or, worse still, that they all sound like you. Perhaps you need to think more carefully about giving each a distinctive voice. You may have fallen into the trap of making characters into mouthpieces whose only real function is to express your own current preoccupations. It's not too late to remedy this but it may mean a complete overhaul of a particular character. You may have to rewrite certain sections or invent new dialogue. For example, you may find that a certain character comes over as rather pale and insignificant when your intention had been to depict her as a powerful personality. If you go through the text you may discover opportunities for her to instigate action rather than react to it. Perhaps you could develop some speeches where she makes outspoken statements and expresses strong emotions. At the same time you could eliminate some of her more anodyne utterances. Look at her first entrance. Does it make a strong impression or have you allowed her to slide into the scene unnoticed?

Ann Jellicoe, in advising about the techniques involved in writing plays for a large cast, stresses the importance of giving every character at least one moment of glory, however modest. All characters, including the minor ones, should have an opportunity to speak out, to lead the action, to change the course of events, even if only in a small way. This moment will create a point of reference for the actor (and thence the audience) and will provide a valuable key.

Always be on the lookout for sexual and racial stereotyping in your own work. However liberal your viewpoint, however raised your consciousness, you will be as prone as we all are to falling heedlessly into the traps created by years of conditioning and the subtle pressure constantly exerted by society. Have you created female characters who are strong in their own right or do they exist merely as foils to their husbands, lovers, fathers? Are your male characters all forceful, dashing and successful? Have they all just stepped out of the pages of a Mills and Boon novel? Or are they able to cry in public, admit defeat, show weakness and prove themselves fallible? Of course, it is equally stereotypical to make all your men violent and villainous and all your women warm, sensitive and caring. Try to think of your characters as individuals rather than rigid examples of certain characteristics.

Look at the extent of individual speeches. Are there a lot of lengthy outbursts? Don't forget that the audience's attention span is limited. Although long speeches can be used effectively, giving a character an opportunity to explore a subject, to present an argument, to push a point of view, it is actually quite unusual, in real life, for someone to be able to speak at any great length without some form of interruption.

Sometimes the interruption itself can act as a spur, goading the speaker on to greater rage, passion or rhetoric.

It's a good idea to aim for variety in the length of speeches. A series of long speeches could send the audience to sleep whereas a sudden lengthy and intense outburst from a character who is normally controlled and terse can be very effective.

Look at the first entrance of every character. Does each one make an individual and distinct impact or do some arrive unannounced and unnoticed? The first impression a character gives to an audience will be similar to the first impressions we give in real life and will be difficult to eradicate. How a character looks when the audience first sees him, what he wears, carries and, most of all, says and does, will all affect the audience's response. Be certain of what you intend and check to see if you have got it right.

Do your characters have sufficient substance or are they wooden, unsubtle or just unconvincing? Perhaps you need to have more information about them to bring them more vividly to life. In the end you may have to concede that a character is totally misconceived, that whatever you thought was interesting or unique about her in the first place has failed to develop.

Rethinking a characterisation is always rather painful and difficult but perseverance can be rewarding. In my first draft of *The Ballad of Tilly Hake* the character of the Ballad Seller failed to convince in any way. Because he was a central figure this failure was causing a serious problem and I could find no simple solution. Ann Jellicoe, with her customary lack of beating about the bush, had a radical idea: "Why don't you make him a her — let the Ballad Seller be a woman!"

It was an extremely effective solution. By making this character a man I had unwittingly blocked much of its potential. But with the Ballad Seller as a woman the real possibilities of interaction between her and Tilly Hake opened up to me. The simple but fundamental change had important reverberations through the entire play and I was able to make a much stronger and clearer statement than before.

Sometimes a completely new character can revolutionise the concept of a play. This happened in *Self Portrait* with the creation of Barbara. In Draft One she didn't exist at all, though she was probably struggling to be born. In Draft Two she emerges as a leading character, the modern counterpart of Gwen John herself, and a strong figure with whom a contemporary audience could easily empathise. The character of Barbara allowed me to move into a new dimension of meaning and gave me an entirely new structure for the play.

First drafts are characteristically lacking in both focus and clarity. When you take a photograph you begin with a general view then you focus in on the particular aspect of the scene you wish to emphasise or explore. The same process can occur in your writing. The reader, and subsequently the audience, should experience a sense of looking at something very close up, able to observe it in all its fine detail. Working towards the second draft is a process of zooming in closer and closer onto your subject. At each reading you bring your text into sharper focus, constantly refining, revising and polishing it.

At first the questions you put to yourself will be fairly general; gradually they will become more and more specific:

You might begin by asking:

▷ Is my intention clear?
▷ Can the audience see what I mean?
▷ Is the progress of the action clear and can it be followed without confusion from start to finish?
▷ Is the motivation of the characters clear?
▷ Does the action spring naturally from the characters?
▷ Is this the most appropriate structure?

Use the 'story-board' technique and the character-analysis exercise when you are considering these questions.

If your play deals in images and metaphors will the audience be able to make sense of what you are saying? It's no good calling the audience stupid or insensitive; if you have a poetic vision it's still your job to communicate effectively. Symbolism that is vague or inadequately developed will fail to deliver the message.

Remember that theatre is a visual medium. The audience will want to see things happen on stage. Your aim should be to create vivid and stirring pictures as well as powerful and sharply defined words. The combination of the two will make exciting theatre. The lack of visual stimulus will make theatre which is dull and lifeless.

Above all, what does your play say? Is it what you meant? If not, is it more than you'd hoped to say or less? If it has failed to meet your aspirations can you understand how the gap has developed and can you find a way of bridging it?

Many first drafts are either too fat or too thin. In the fat first draft you have poured everything onto the blank page. You have clearly been hoarding all this material for years and now it has all come out with little restraint or self-censorship. It's an incredible feast of words, startling in its sheer abundance. At the end of writing such a first draft you will feel exhausted, strangely vindicated, and possibly quite stunned by the number of words you have managed to produce.

It is likely that you have enough here for several plays. A careful and objective read-through will reveal many different themes struggling for recognition within a mass of rich but as yet unfocussed material. Hidden inside all this there may well be an excellent play but you will have to prune away a lot of extraneous stuff to discover it. You will, of course, hate to reject one single word of what you've fought so hard to realise but only when you are prepared to pare down what you've written will a viable play emerge.

Ask yourself: "What is the central theme?" There are probably several. Perhaps you can single one out as more significant than the others. If you can, you may decide to cut away those aspects of the text that aren't directly connected with that theme. They needn't be wasted; you can retain the 'clippings' and maybe develop them into independent pieces of work later on.

First plays, and particularly first drafts of first plays, often contain a bit of everything. They may be tangled and undisciplined but it is an intriguing and glorious mess, a colourful rag-bag of all the ideas which have inhabited your brain through all the barren wordless years. Putting these ideas on paper is, in itself, an act of rejoicing, a wonderful release, a valuable recognition of their value. It was good to do it and you will have benefited enormously. But now, convinced that you can write because you *have* written, you can afford to look at the material a little more dispassionately and to consider its specific potential as writing for the theatre.

Is your play intrinsically dramatic? Some writers think they want to write a play but, on completing the first draft, find that they have written a short story with dialogue or an embryonic novel. If you make this discovery about your work don't regard it as a defeat: it's a valuable realisation. You won't waste what you've written since it can obviously provide the basis for further work in a different form.

Up to the point of writing the world of your play existed only in your imagination. Now it is there on paper and may soon be scrutinised by actors, a director and, subsequently, an audience.

Although you may have the opportunity of explaining your thought processes to those who work on your text it will almost certainly be impossible to give them more than a brief insight into the intricate workings of your imagination. The text must speak for itself from now on, without your intercession. Nor will you be there every night in the theatre to explain the finer points to the audience; the play must stand or fall on its own merits.

It's hard for a writer to adjust to the fact that, although she may see everything as clear as crystal, what she has actually put on the page is somehow less clear or open to misinterpretation. A good director can help a writer to clarify what she has written but for the moment you must be your own judge and critic.

One sometimes hears writers described as self-indulgent; it's a crime of which we are all guilty from time to time. In terms of a stage play I think it means forgetting the needs of the audience.

If you imagine that everything you have written is wonderful, that everything you have experienced is fascinating, and that anyone who doesn't appreciate every word of it is automatically stupid, then you will run the risk of behaving like the worst kind of bore at a party, the one who collars you in a corner and launches into his interminable story. He doesn't care whether you are interested; he doesn't know whether you are listening. Like the Ancient Mariner he talks because he feels compelled to. You will feel bored, resentful and angry and, at the first possible opportunity, you will escape.

The art in writing generally is to learn to select from the mass of material available to you that which is most telling, most interesting and most appropriate. The art in writing for the theatre is to present that material in its most dramatic form. You have to capture the imagination and attention of the audience and hold it till you have finished your story.

Far from being vastly overblown a thin first draft is undernourished and underdeveloped. Perhaps the play feels very short. I say 'feels', because it is not necessarily related to the actual number of words or scenes. A short play can still be complete and perfectly satisfying while a longer play may feel unfinished. It's a question of whether you have explored the full potential of your subject or whether you have skimmed the surface, leaving vast areas undiscovered and unexplored.

Perhaps there are scenes which begin bravely but rapidly fizzle out or characters who have nothing much to say and even less to do.

Because you have been carrying your ideas in your imagination for a while you may think that you have written everything down. But you may find that those ideas are still in your head and not on the paper at all.

Where the fat draft needs stripping down to the bone to reveal its true character the thin draft needs to be fleshed out. This isn't just a question of padding. You aren't going to add to it only in bulk but also in texture and richness. Look first at the whole. Does it explore many aspects of the subject or is it all on one note? Are there scenes which could be more fully developed or places where a new scene might add a different dimension? Have you missed opportunities for visual set-pieces which could add depth and variety?

Are the characters drawn with detail and subtlety or are they sketchy and lacking in definition? Could you perhaps insert new scenes to throw fresh light on a character? Imagine a scene in which a normally cheerful man shows a more sombre side or one where a quiet and withdrawn woman becomes brighter and more extrovert.

Is there sufficient action or does very little really happen? Is there the potential for developing new incidents or a sub-plot? It's probably less painful to build a play up than to cut it down; it's a process which feels very constructive whereas the act of cutting back can seem like a sort of bereavement.

Some first drafts are neither too fat nor too thin. They are simply too tight, held too firmly in the writer's control. Stuffed to the gills with material, the text can't breathe and nor can the reader. You long for a moment to relax, to be let off the hook. In these texts everything is explained, spelt out and hammered home. The writer is a bully, holding the reader (and potentially the audience) by the scruff of the neck, intimidating and haranguing. It will be hard for you to admit that you have written this kind of first draft, particularly if you are still in the grip of the fear which made you do it. You were afraid that no one would understand what you meant so you have spelled it out in words of one syllable. You were afraid that it isn't really all that important or worth saying so you puffed it up with serious-sounding speeches or with academic references. You were afraid that the characters would get loose like circus animals on the rampage so you kept them on a very short rein and gave them little opportunity to express themselves.

This kind of first draft may be in need of urgent and radical surgery but it will probably take a while for you to accept the fact. You will be more than usually defensive of it, convinced that it is an absolute masterpiece and ready to send it out to directors or theatre companies exactly as it stands. Relax a little. Put it to one side for a week or so, then return to it and read it through at one sitting. You may be shocked and surprised to find that it bores you. You get to page fifty-four and you find yourself sneaking a look to see how many more pages there are. It lacks vitality, reading more like an essay or a diatribe than a play. What you thought you were writing and what you actually wrote are clearly not the same thing.

Recognising the gap between what you saw in your mind's eye and what is actually there on the page is a difficult and sobering task.

Perhaps you have been too ambitious or not ambitious enough. Perhaps what seemed very fascinating as an abstract idea looks disappointingly less interesting when transformed into a play.

But don't give up. Ask yourself the key question and wait for an answer. What is the *real* subject of the play you have written? Not the obvious subject, not what you thought was the subject, but what hooked you into it in the first instance, what attracted you to it and propelled you through it?

I was convinced that my play *A Quieter Sort of Battle* was just a play about two women, one young, one old, meeting in an empty house. But it turns out to be a play about mothers and daughters; the sub-text is all about the difficulties of finding common ground between the two generations and the pain which that produces.

The real subject of your play may well have remained hidden from you up to this point. You may have successfully convinced yourself that you were an innocent and objective observer of the events you portrayed. Now you may have to admit to a more personal involvement with your material in order to penetrate to a deeper level of its meaning.

In *Geraniums* I thought I was writing about an historic event in the 1930's. By Draft Three I had admitted to and dared to explore the real subject: the gap between youthful idealism and the harsh realities and subsequent cynicism which often pervade old age. I started off with a tightly held, rather academic, piece which described events, then worked slowly towards a much more fluid play in which I explored feelings and looked closely at my own reaction to situations which were both painful and intimate. In the first draft I was working from the outside looking in; in the later draft I was very much inside the characters, trying to understand what it was to be them and to experience events as they did.

Here is part of a letter I wrote to Anne Challenor, one of the workshop students, after reading the first draft of her play:

Mirror Image:
"I'm going to be quite radical about this because I want you to reconsider the true subject and therefore the structure of the play. At present I feel a sense of attending a seminar about the subject, and a certain knowledge that, beneath the rational lurks an altogether more untidy and dramatic play.

Perhaps it's about 'stripping down', cutting away a lot of the dialectic to reveal the *personal* underneath.

I feel that what is interesting about this piece is what is peculiar/par cular/ specific about *this* relationship, not what is general or common to many situations . . ."

Quite understandably, Anne found these notes difficult to take on board. She had worked extremely hard on the first draft and now I had the audacity to suggest a radical restructuring of the whole play in an attempt to expose the true subject, which was at that point hidden inside the rather formal framework. But she decided to try what I suggested. What emerged in the second draft was altogether more exciting, more dramatic and considerably more powerful.

If you are in a workshop or similar group you may be encouraged to show your first draft. If, like me, you have written it in a pencilled scribble on an A4 pad, this may not be a viable possibility. What you present will, in these circumstances, be your second draft, a neater version of the first and possibly the outcome of a certain degree of revision, but still far from finished.

If you are working on a word processor, or if you have typed your first draft, you may be tempted to show it to all and sundry. This could be a mistake. Your play is still in an embryonic state, fluid and extremely fragile. It is all too easy to destroy it. There is no such thing as objective criticism. Often those who are closest to you will find it hardest to look at your work without prejudice. You show your play to your husband. You have written scenes of domestic violence. Your husband is not a violent man so he is subconsciously affronted by the implied critique of masculine behaviour. But what he says is: "Don't like the character of Jack. Found him rather one-dimensional."

At a later stage you will, of course, be forced to expose your work to criticism, misunderstanding and attack. But by then you should be standing on firmer ground and should feel strong enough to withstand the blows, or at least survive them. At present the best judge of what you have written is you.

When the relief and euphoria at finishing the first draft have subsided you may experience a severe and crippling loss of confidence. You read and re-read what you have written and it all seems completely meaningless, without a single redeeming feature. How could you ever have imagined that you had anything worth saying? Whatever possessed you to think that you could write? Your first impulse is to tear it all up and throw it into the waste paper basket. Please don't.

What you are experiencing is an inevitable and natural separation from what you have written. Before you could start writing it was essential to work yourself up into a kind of frenzy in order to find the passion and energy necessary to begin at all. Whilst you were working on the first draft you were borne along on a tide of excitement and expectation and a very understandable desire to reach the end. Now comes a deep sense of anti-climax. The work is no longer inside you, an intrinsic and inseparable part of you: it has an external existence; it *is* in its own right. The objectivity required to take you from the first to the second draft may temporarily have the effect of cancelling out your fierce sense of identification with your play. It may suddenly seem ugly rather than beautiful, the words may sound empty and pointless rather than vitally important and worthy of expression. Don't destroy it or abandon it. Understand what is happening and try to live through it. Take a few days or weeks to acclimatise yourself to the idea that your play is *there* — that it is something you can pick up and look at, that it is no longer a part of you but exists in that pile of paper sitting on your desk. Then approach it kindly, cautiously, and without too much prejudice. Try to read it as if someone else had written it. It will be an interesting experience.

Never destroy what you have written, however much you hate it and feel like rejecting it. Put it away and come back to it. One day you may find that it will provide an excellent basis for an entirely new piece of work.

Better still, stick with it and try to find a way to make it more closely resemble what you had originally intended. Go back to your research notes, remind yourself of what you had in mind, try to stir up some of your original excitement. Try to understand how what you have written has diverged specifically from what you wanted to write and consider why this has happened.

Destroying a piece of work won't eradicate it. It will be there to haunt you for ages. You will wonder what it might have become, given the chance. You will regret and mourn its passing.

The transition from the first to the second draft is a very delicate stage in the process of writing a play. Your willingness to make that transition will show that you understand that writing is part inspiration and part craft and that it is the fusion of the two which creates a satisfying and viable piece of work.

CHAPTER EIGHT

Into the Second Draft –
A Workshop Reading

– Cutting the text – Organising a reading –
– Letting go – Working with a director –
– The preliminary read-through – The rehearsed reading –
– The post-mortem – Taking notes – Revising the text –

Now that you have finished the second draft, having expended a great deal of time and energy to bring the text to its present state, there seems little more you can do until you have some informed feedback.

The elation and excitement which you experienced at the end of the first draft have drained away, leaving you uneasily becalmed and vaguely depressed. Perhaps you are beginning to realise that an important part of the process is over, that this secret which you have carried inside you for so long, which was your private passion and most personal possession, is soon to become public property. Naturally this induces a feeling of impending loss. Writing a play is a little like carrying a baby to full term and then painfully giving birth. Now you have reached the stage where your child is almost ready to face the world, to be exposed to the critical and unloving eyes of others. It will be removed from your constant vigilance and protection and forced to stand on its own two feet.

Before you show the play to anyone at all you obviously want to make sure that it looks good and can give the strongest possible account of itself.

Although you will almost certainly feel incapable of deciding on any major changes to the text you should try to give it a very careful reading with a view to making cuts and small adjustments. Perhaps at this read-through you will find individual words or sentences which are insufficiently specific. Or you may discover whole passages which seem extraneous, repetitious or over-long. Cutting your text unaided is never easy but it's a good idea to train your eye to spot superfluous material, or any signs of obvious over-writing or padding, and to eradicate them at this stage.

Once you have read the text through once and made these cuts, read it through again, conducting a more detailed search for single words which aren't necessary. Cut any word which doesn't have a definite purpose; it's surprising how they can hold up the flow of the dialogue. Innocuous little words like 'well', and 'but', 'Yes and . . .' 'Yes but . . .' are usually quite ineffectual. Writers sometimes justify them by describing them as colloquial but all they do is slow things down. Every word should be razor-sharp, vital. Every word should work for its living. If it doesn't, cut it.

It's good to learn to be quite ruthless in this process, even if it means waving goodbye to your favourite passage of purple prose, your most lovingly crafted descriptive passage, your most heartfelt outburst. If a speech strikes you as boring, wordy or pointless, imagine how it will strike the audience. I would advise you to do your own cutting; other people will be far less sentimental about your precious words than you are.

Don't throw away the passages you cut. You may have second thoughts at a later stage. A reading or a production could reveal that the cut passages were, after all, significant, and you may decide to reinstate them.

If you have any serious misgivings about the text as a whole I doubt whether you will have the mental energy to motivate yourself into a third draft without first seeking the opinion of someone who will be able to offer constructive and informed advice.

Writers are, by nature, fragile, and this is a particularly vulnerable time for you. You need someone who can assess your play without destroying it (and you) completely. How can you find out whether the play works at all, works only in places, needs a complete overhaul, or just some minor adjustments? If it doesn't work, who will advise you what to do to make it work? If it does work, but could work better, who can suggest how to make it more effective?

I have recently shown a second draft of a play to several friends who know my work well. In so doing I broke with my normal practice of never showing anyone anything. I did it because I felt particularly confused and insecure about what I had written and desperately needed some feedback before deciding what could be done to improve the text. Each friend read the play with love and great care. Each gave me a detailed response — all different. Even accounting for the personal prejudices, widely varied experience and viewpoint of each reader, it was hard to find a common thread in their reactions. All I could deduce, without a shadow of a doubt, was that the play needed a further draft.

Whatever you do, don't send your play out to theatres at this stage: it isn't ready. If you do send it out, the chances are higher than usual that it will be rejected. This is not because it's a bad play but because, almost certainly, it is still work in progress. Of course, theatres should be sensitive to the potential of new plays, should not demand a 'finished' text, but should be happy to see work which, with care and support, could be developed to production. Directors should be happy to nurse new and inexperienced writers, coaxing them to improve on and develop the early drafts of their plays till they ripen into work of greater power and subtlety. And pigs should grow wings and take to the skies.

The reality is that all theatres are severely underfunded; very few have anyone whose specific job it is to foster new work. Artistic directors wrestle daily with the practical problems of keeping afloat in increasingly hostile waters whilst at the same time trying to produce good work.

Though new writing is the life-blood of the theatre and your work, once brought to fruition, may well be the most exciting and challenging play imaginable, very few theatres regard work on undeveloped or emerging texts as a top priority.

Having read a great many first or early plays, my feeling is that the best way forward at this stage is to hear the play read aloud, preferably under the guidance of an experienced director, and using experienced actors who have some commitment to the ideals of fostering new writing.

The 'Made in Wales' workshops culminated in a weekend spent working with actors and director Gilly Adams. The aim of this was to explore and develop the plays written by the women and to stimulate further work on the texts in order to make them more viable for full production. For most of the women it was their first contact with a professional director and actors and, as such, was both a daunting and an exciting prospect.

I consider it a vital part of the process of writing a play to expose the text for the first time in supportive surroundings in order to see how it will lift off the page and come alive. The eye of an experienced director, used to working with emerging text, and the active participation of actors who are also familiar with work in progress, are important components of the experience for the writers concerned.

These weekends did not culminate in a public reading — they were solely for the benefit of the writers. Therefore, the process lacked the final component: the audience. But, since an audience is, by definition, a group of people prepared to watch and react, then the actors, the other writers and I formed an ad hoc audience for each piece and were able to give some impression of what the response of a real audience might be.

If you are a member of a writing workshop or group it should not be too difficult to set up such a reading. If you are working alone you may have to look further afield. To find out about workshops in your area, try the public library, adult education centres or your local theatre.

Whereas productions are expensive to mount, a reading is relatively cheap. And in the present economic climate many experienced and often-produced writers are finding themselves grateful for a public reading of a new piece of work where once they might have hoped for a full-scale production. Regard a reading not as an end in itself but as a means of developing your text with a view to offering it to a theatre when you feel it is finally ready.

Failing all else, you could always arrange a reading in your own home, inviting friends or local actors who might be prepared to work with you in return for a stimulating evening and a good meal.

Your play is about to pass out of your hands for the first time. The text will be read and digested by a director who will then try to cast it with actors who are appropriate to play the characters you have invented.

An audience, however modest, will hear the play, and be in a position to give their response. A rehearsed reading will give a reasonable impression of how a text will work in production. If a play stands up well without the benefit of costume, set or music, it is a fair indication that the text is good. A reading may also expose aspects of the text which need to be developed, changed or cut, and reveal defects in characterisation or plot.

The term 'workshop' implies that, before a polished reading is given, some work will be done on the text by both actors and writer. Sometimes directors will allow several days for this process, sometimes just a few hours. This enables the writer to see the play 'on its feet' and to make on-the-spot decisions regarding changes to the text before the reading takes place.

The important thing is that a workshop and reading are principally for the benefit of the writer. Although it may have a public face, in that an audience will be brought in at the end to see the result of the process, the workshop is specifically designed to enable you to do further work on your text. It is a recognition of the fact that a play has no real existence until it is brought to life in three dimensions. It is a valuable and instructive means of lifting your text off the page and holding it up for your close scrutiny.

Writing for the theatre is by its nature a collaborative art. Up to this point you have written in total isolation but beyond this point you must learn to work in conjunction with those who can help to bring your text to life before an audience. Letting go of your play for the first time will be traumatic, however supportive the surroundings, however sensitive the other participants. Even if you have prepared yourself or have been prepared for the experience, handing your play over, first to a director, and subsequently to actors, will be both extraordinarily exciting and extremely painful.

Never underestimate the difficulty of sharing your work, of exposing it to the scrutiny of others and the pain when it is misunderstood or misinterpreted, the sense of disappointment or defeat when it fails to communicate what you have felt so passionately.

Most experienced writers are frightened of directors and terrified of actors. Working with a director for the first time won't be easy but it will help if you understand the nature of the relationship.

The first thing to remember is that the writer and the director are equals. Very often the new writer feels at a distinct disadvantage when working with an experienced director; most directors are sensitive to this but some may capitalise on it. The result will be an uneasy relationship which is uncomfortable for both parties and detrimental to the work in hand.

The director's job, whether in workshop reading or production, is to serve your text, to interpret it and bring it to life as vividly and as powerfully as possible. The text is yours — it had no life of any kind before you called it into existence — and so you have a perfect right to ask that it should be presented as you envisaged. A good director will try to understand and empathise with your intentions and, by questioning you exhaustively about the text, assure herself that you have carried them out. She will look at the text with utmost care, trying to understand all that is there, looking for the best means of communicating your ideas to the audience.

In the workshop process, as in a full-scale production, the best results will be achieved by a harmonious collaboration between writer and director. It is the director's responsibility to be aware of your vulnerability and to work with you to draw the very best from your text. It is your responsibility to safeguard the integrity of what you have written whilst at the same time opening yourself up to all genuine attempts to improve it. If the director bullies, you will recoil. If you are totally inflexible, the director will have no room for manoeuvre. Director and writer should aim to build a relationship of mutual trust, which must be based on a belief in the validity of the text. It is hard for a director to work on a play which she mistrusts or dislikes.

The director will be concerned with interpreting what you have written to the actors, in order that they, in turn, may interpret it to the audience. If the text is not clear the director may ask you to clarify it. If it meanders she may ask you to cut it. If a character lacks substance she may ask you to build on it.

The writer must learn to tread a narrow line between pig-headed obstinacy and total unquestioning acquiescence. Don't regard the director's questions or suggestions as threats to your autonomy. They may usefully expose gaps or inconsistencies in the text and provide you with the means of rectifying them. On the other hand, don't automatically agree to every change, especially if you don't see the justification for it. The director may be wrong: she may have mis-read or misunderstood the text. If you don't want to change it, don't. Never agree to even the most minor changes unless you honestly feel that they are an improvement. If you feel at all uncertain, then reserve the right to see what happens at the reading.

If the director seems to misunderstand much of what you have written you must ask youself whether it is because it isn't clear or because she hasn't read it properly. Don't jump to the conclusion that you are at fault, nor assume automatically that she is.

The fact that you have carried all this in your head for a long time may make you myopic. You may be quite incapable of acknowledging any problem in your play. But, while nobody understands your intentions better than you, the director will probably have more direct experience of what is theatrical and so may be able to suggest ways of clarifying those intentions to an audience.

In a full-scale production you would expect a high degree of involvement in the choice of both director and actors. In the case of a workshop reading you will probably have little choice.

Some companies with a policy of encouraging new writing have a pool of actors who are prepared to work for small remuneration for the interest and stimulation of being actively involved with work which is still in progress.

If there is a particular actor you like or who lives in your area, you may be able to request that she be asked to read the part you consider suitable. But don't expect stars, household names or television personalities to give up their Sunday afternoon for the honour of reading your play.

When you first set eyes on the actors who are to play the characters you have created you will probably be bitterly disappointed. For weeks, or perhaps months, you have held these people in your mind's eye till they have grown more familiar to you than friends or family. You feel that you know exactly what they look like, every line in the face, every hair on the head. You know how tall they are, the colour of their eyes, the tone of their voice. Now you are faced with real people who, however closely they may resemble the characters you have imagined, can never be perfect replicas of them.

The actors, in turn, will be pleased (or not so pleased) with the part they have to play. Every actor longs for the part which fits like a glove, which stretches her to the utmost of her ability, which enables her to show the full range of her skills. Perhaps the part you have written is less exciting than she had hoped; perhaps it seems limited or stereotyped. Yet she must work with whatever is there on the page; her job is not to invent but to interpret. She can only operate within the confines of the part you have written.

You may find yourself developing an instant empathy with one actor, feeling that she is absolutely right for your character, whilst another will evoke a less positive response: she doesn't look right, she doesn't sound right, she lacks the qualities you had in mind.

One major difference between an informal workshop and a full-scale production process is that in a workshop you will undoubtedly have closer personal contact with the actors. In rehearsal for a production most directors prefer the writer to communicate with the actors through them. This is because the whole activity is moving towards the end product: the public performance. The director will be concerned with results, with building up unity and confidence in her cast and with maintaining some kind of authority in order to keep control of the process.

A workshop, with or without a public reading, has a different emphasis. Its main concern is process; it is seen primarily as a means of allowing the writer to perfect the text, with the help of director and actors. You will find that discussion with actors and consideration of their reactions both to their own characters and to the play as a whole will throw a great deal of light on the text and may provide you with much useful information.

Most workshops begin with a preliminary read-through. Before this the director may ask you to say something about how the play came to be written. This is to help the actors by providing background information and giving them a sense of how your initial involvement with the subject evolved. This is an opportunity to share anything about the research process or the gradual development of the original idea which may throw light on the play. But don't be tempted to apologise or explain too much; even in these circumstances the play must stand up for itself.

The first time you hear your play read aloud you will probably feel disappointed. Actors may struggle with unfamiliar vocabulary; accents may not sound right. It may seem dull, flat and uninteresting. But don't jump to conclusions; this is only the very beginning of the process of bringing the text to life.

After the first read-through the director may encourage the actors to question you in turn about their characters. This is to help them to flesh out what is on the page, to clarify any doubts or misapprehensions. It may also begin to reveal to you gaps in the text.

Don't assume, however, that every critical comment exposes a real gap in your writing. You may be right and the actor wrong. On the other hand, do not ignore what the actors say. Make a note of every question left unanswered and every major criticism or radical suggestion. The reading may have quickly uncovered a problem in the text which you may be able to resolve with the actors' help.

Depending on the duration of the workshop, the director may suggest some work designed to help solve any difficulties which have been revealed. Perhaps a problematical scene can be looked at in detail, examining exactly what happens and how.

Some directors suggest that, if the dialogue seems strained or wooden, it may help the writer if the actors improvise around it, using their own imaginations to create further dialogue. This won't necessarily form any part of the revised text but it may give you some fresh ideas which you could incorporate at a later stage.

If there is a whole day or a weekend in which to work on the play the director may even suggest some on-the-spot repair to the text.

If you are a writer who can work quickly you may feel excited at the prospect of reacting to the stimulus provided by the actors and may eagerly settle down to some rapid rewriting, suffused with new energy and ideas. Other writers curl up and die when faced with this sort of situation. For them the writing process is essentially very private so they may find it impossible to respond to quick-fire suggestions.

Whilst I am a very slow and extremely secretive writer I have sometimes enjoyed responding to the challenge presented by actors in a workshop situation, finding the work pushed on beyond my original conception by an influx of fresh ideas. After the intense isolation of the writing process it can be refreshing to work in a spontaneous, more open way. Don't forget that, after the workshop is over, you will have the opportunity to reconsider the changes you have made and to decide whether they constitute a real improvement.

Directors often ask the writer for cuts. You don't have to agree to these but it always makes sense to consider them seriously. An experienced director will have a strong sense of how a piece will affect an audience.

She will see where you have overstated your case, repeated yourself or included material which isn't interesting or relevant.

Most writers hate cutting. You should never submit to cuts which you don't understand or with which you disagree. You may be right and the director may be wrong. If you are unsure about cuts, say that you need time to think about them.

During a workshop a certain actor may be particularly critical of the play. If he is sensitive to the needs of an inexperienced writer the criticism will be constructive and aimed at helping you to clarify your thoughts. But sometimes criticism is destructive and painful.

Actors are as fragile as writers. They are also very interested in the part they have to play. If that part isn't working for them they will feel threatened and exposed and, if a public reading is to follow, concerned about how the audience will react. The writer who has put them in this hot-spot is the obvious scapegoat for all their fears. This is where the director can protect you from unjustified attack.

The most important thing to remember is that the text is not set in concrete. However complete you feel it is your play is still in a fluid state and will remain so till it receives a full production and possibly even beyond that point. A play text is constantly evolving, in response to directors, actors, audience and to your own developing awarenes of what will and won't work in theatrical terms. Keep a flexible mind; be prepared to see how things work out in practice. Be open to changes at any stage in the process.

A rehearsed reading was arranged for my play *Free 'n' Lovely* prior to the full production scheduled for it by Theatre Venture in Stratford East. The reading, which was preceded by a full day's rehearsal, was followed by a lively discussion involving both actors and audience. The text, as it stood, included the surprise appearance of a gun, which I considered both dramatic and daring. The actor required to use the gun thought otherwise; the audience agreed with him. Intense debate gradually persuaded me away from my original idea towards a somewhat more subtle solution. In the final text there was no sign of a gun.

Jane Buckler's play, *Burd Mary,* later performed by 'Made in Wales', was written in the first series of workshops. By the weekend of the readings it was still very fluid in form. Jane felt that there was more work to be done but was unsure how to proceed.

After the play had been read through once, the director Gilly Adams began to work in detail on certain scenes with the actors, drawing out their meaning, coaxing the characters into life. She and the actors approached the text with sensitivity and in a spirit of enquiry so that all kinds of possibilities rapidly emerged. Jane didn't feel threatened or bullied, rather endorsed and encouraged by their participation and interest.

It's always exciting for a writer to see the unexplored potential of a text and usually has the effect of stimulating further work.

Anne Challenor's play, *Mirror Image*, still had certain structural problems when it was read at the weekend. Nevertheless, the subject matter was taken very seriously by everyone present and the play provoked lengthy discussion. I think this in itself is validating to an inexperienced writer. Anne saw that her text, even if still unresolved, had the power to stimulate debate and she had the satisfaction of seeing the characters she had created capturing the imagination of the actors who played them.

It's always astonishing for a writer when she sees her characters come to life but for Pat Lewis, whose play *Iron Them Dry* was totally autobiographical, it was a both moving and painful experience. The actor chosen to play her father almost certainly looked nothing like the real man and the actress who was to play her mother probably bore little resemblance to her actual mother. Pat quickly had to learn that, however closely based on fact, a play is a work of fiction; the actor's job is to create a character for an audience that have never known his real-life counterpart. Facial or even vocal similarity is less important than the ability to capture the essence. In spite of the writer's natural desire to instruct the actors how to imitate the real people they portrayed, in the end it was the text which had to provide the essential information.

If the workshop culminates in a public reading you will have the added benefit of a real audience to respond to your work. You will not have to wait till the end of the play to gauge the audience's reaction to it. You can tell, by watching faces and body language, how it is going right from the start. You may have considered the play wildly funny: the audience may disagree. You may have thought it deeply tragic: the audience may be moved to laughter instead of tears.

Don't rush to condemn the audience if they fail to appreciate what you have written. Don't berate them for their lack of humour if they don't laugh at all your jokes. Don't blame the director and the actors if the play doesn't produce a positive response. The real value of a workshop and reading is that it will let you see what still needs to be done and give you some indication of how to do it. But the experience can only be valuable to you if you are open to its possibilities and ready to absorb what it can teach you.

It may be helpful to have a mental check-list for assessing how well the play is working in its present state.

▷ Did all the characters come to life?

▷ Did each actor seem satisfied with the part she/he had to play or was any actor unable to translate your intentions into a performance?

▷ Did any character seem less well-developed than the rest, surprisingly unsympathetic, less amusing or powerful than you had hoped?

▷ Did the actors experience difficulty in speaking the lines? If so, maybe the structure of speeches was awkward, the vocabulary unfamiliar, the syntax unnecessarily complex, the rhythm stilted.

▷ Was the story easy to follow or did the audience seem confused?

▷ Was the audience absorbed and willingly drawn into the world you had created or were they distracted, restless or bored?

▷ Did the overall mood of the play come over as you had intended?

▷ Did people laugh where you'd hoped they would or was there an embarrassed silence?

▷ Did the audience giggle or suppress a yawn just where you thought events had reached their dramatic climax?

With or without an audience you will probably find a workshop a powerful and difficult experience and you will need time to absorb all its implications.

Although everyone will try hard to be constructive and gentle in their criticism you may feel overwhelmed by a barrage of often conflicting comment. One person says: "Cut the third act". Another suggests the introduction of a completely new character. A third thinks you should set the whole play in the future. It's a little like being pulled apart by a pack of well-intentioned wolves.

Allow a little time for the dust to settle. Make some notes about the salient points raised during the workshop. Ask yourself as honestly as you can whether you feel that, in broad terms, the play worked. If not, what are its major defects? Look at all the comments and suggestions and see if you can detect a common thread, a repeated theme. Do you agree with the most commonly voiced criticism? Is there a practical way forward?

Sometimes what is needed is some drastic cutting or some careful rewriting. It may be possible to rewrite part of a scene, or part of several scenes, in order to rectify an imbalance in the action or to clear up some confusion. Cutting may reveal the shape of the play more clearly and clarify what seemed obscure.

Perhaps the workshop has convinced you that a particular character needs to be built up. This may be achieved without too much upheaval by giving her additional speeches at certain key points in the action or even devising one or two new scenes in which she will figure prominently.

You are faced with a difficult decision. Will minor and manageable rewrites, additions or deletions produce a satisfactory text, or is there something so intrinsically wrong with plot or characterisation that only a major overhaul will produce results?

Sometimes a workshop reading will give you a sudden and startling insight. You will see in a flash that an entire dimension was lacking from your concept of the play. You will feel instinctively that if you could only add that dimension then the whole play would open out.

This, of course, means a Third Draft. The prospect may be too daunting and you may prefer to put the play to one side, imperfect as it is, and move on to the next project.

Or, fired with new enthusiasm, you may draw a long, deep breath, and return to the text with renewed energy and commitment. You may regard it almost as if it were a new piece of work.

It is not at all unusual for my plays to go into three drafts, sometimes more. But I know that, for new writers, the hundred yards dash holds more appeal than the marathon. For that reason I never try to persuade a writer to continue with a piece of work once the energy has gone out of it.

But sometimes you feel so revitalised by contact with actors and director, so inspired by the as yet unexplored potential of your play, that nothing can stop you from embarking on a completely new and improved version of the text.

If this is how you feel, that's fine. If it isn't, then content yourself with minor adjustments, further fine cutting, and whatever changes you can make without undertaking a major restructuring of the text.

Your play may still go through many changes if and when it is offered a production. But, for the moment, because you have done as much work on it as you feel you can, it is finished.

CHAPTER NINE

The Finished Play – Seeking a Production

– Finding a theatre – Approaching a director –
– The role of the literary agent – Coping with rejection –
– Coping with acceptance – Negotiating a contract – Casting –
– The designer – Rehearsals – The first night –
– Audience reaction – The critics –
– Coming down to earth – Publication –

Having guided you as realistically as I can through the long and often difficult process of writing your play it would be dishonest of me to suggest that this, the final stage, will be any easier than what has gone before.

The business of sending work out to theatres or directors can prove both painful and demoralising for all writers, however experienced they are. I can't spare you the pain, because it is an intrinsic part of being a writer, but I would like to offer some suggestions on how to survive the process.

We live in a society which places little value on the artist, however prominent, brilliant or prolific. We live in a time when theatres are forced to close because of inadequate subsidy and touring companies are driven off the road, deprived of grants. Faced with ever dwindling resources those theatres which remain have their backs to the wall. They must justify their existence in terms of box office, must go cap in hand to industry and private sponsorship for support, and must look for product which, by dint of its popular appeal, might magically reverse their financial fortunes.

The Royal Shakespeare Company and the Royal National Theatre mount American musicals; the hope of a West End transfer burns brightly in the eye of every fringe management; artistic directors are forced to divert their talents into fund-raising and administration.

You are an unknown writer. This is your first play. It may be astonishing, important, original, of enormous potential value and interest to an audience starved of exciting and challenging work. We are told (against the hard evidence) that new work is not good box office, that audiences are nervous to commit their time or money to the work of a playwright they've never heard of.

When you send your script to a theatre it not only starts out with this disadvantage, it is also one of hundreds of unsolicited scripts by other writers like yourself, all vying for the attention of one director with a pitifully small budget.

I have based this book on the assumption that you wanted passionately to write a play, that you needed to write a play, and that nothing would stop you. I considered it important to encourage you to write the play you wanted to write rather than attempt to give you a blueprint for the type of play most likely to find favour.

There is, anyway, no magic formula for writing a play which will automatically be adopted. Factors such as personal taste, expediency, fashion and prejudice, as well as obvious financial considerations, will all colour a theatre's choice of material for production.

If your play has a huge cast it will probably stand less of a chance than if it has a cast of three. If it deals with an issue which is currently very topical it may catch the eye of a director. But there are exceptions to every rule. An issue can be seen as over-exposed. "Oh dear, not another anti-nuclear play!" and "Well, we've already done a play by a woman," are both statements I've heard with my own ears.

One possible approach is to engage in some market research in an attempt to target a theatre whose programme seems to include plays similar in tone, form or content to the play you have written. This might at least help to minimise frustration and wasted postage. If a theatre seems to specialise in Whitehall-type farces, re-runs of Agatha Christie thrillers and Noel Coward revivals it is unlikely that it will suddenly develop a consuming interest in your searing and controversial drama.

A list of regional theatres such as Bristol Old Vic, Derby Playhouse, Theatre Royal, York, The Swan at Worcester, the Sherman Theatre, Cardiff, can be found in *The Writer's Handbook*, together with addresses and names of contacts.

Another approach is to try to establish a connection with a particular freelance director whose work strikes a chord with you and whose choice of plays seems to indicate that your own work might appeal. The names of many theatre directors are to be found in the *British Alternative Theatre Directory*.

Alternatively, you could introduce yourself to a touring company whose work you have seen and admired, and ask them if they would like to read your play. The disadvantage of this is that these companies often try to commission work specifically tailored to their requirements. Your play may not have a suitable cast or may not satisfy the strenuous and particular requirements of touring, such as straightforward sets and costumes and a particularly accessible text if the company tours to many non-theatrical venues.

There is, of course, nothing to stop you sending your work to any theatre or any director, including the major national companies. Your play could be the very thing they are looking for. If you are prepared for rejection and promise not to be defeated by it then there is no harm in aiming for the stars. First plays have been performed at illustrious venues and chosen by famous directors. Yours could be the next.

Coming down to earth, you could send your script to one of the good fringe venues in London such as the Bush, the Soho Poly or The Orange Tree. The addresses of these and other similar small theatres are listed in *The Writer's Handbook*.

Small venues like these have an excellent reputation for producing exciting new work and are able to attract the very best directors and actors, as well as a committed audience. You would be fortunate to have your play accepted by any of them.

After two years of intensive writing, endless hours spent at the photo-copier, and a depressing number of rejections, I had my first two short plays, *A Quieter Sort of Battle* and *98 Days to Xmas*, accepted for production at The Orange Tree in Richmond in 1979.

Directed by Julia Pascal, the plays provoked quite favourable audience reaction and were reviewed in the national press. This signalled neither fame nor fortune but at least it allowed me to begin to take myself a little more seriously as a playwright.

Unfortunately, in the current climate, there are not many fringe theatres in a position to mount their own productions of new work. Instead, they often ask a director to pay for the use of their space to put on a play. This will, of course, place an extra onus on the play to make money at the box office as the director and company have to cover their own costs.

I am often asked whether it is worth entering playwriting competitions. I have to say that they seem to me like cattle markets or lotteries and tend to raise false hopes but I do know that writing to a specific deadline can be an encouragement and stimulus to some writers. It is important to remember that most competitions attract enormous entries and so any one individual's hopes of success are slim.

Will it help if you have an agent? Well, it might, but it is unlikely that you will be able to get one for your first play. An agent's job is to try to promote your work in exchange for a percentage – usually 10% – of your earnings. For this she will negotiate contracts, set up meetings with people who may express interest in your work, attempt to find a market for your plays, and generally act as an intermediary between you and the theatrical establishment.

Although many writers enjoy, as I do, a friendly and informal relationship with their agent, it is a business relationship, And an inexperienced playwright is not a very valuable commodity. Once your play has been performed and rapturously received by audience and critics, you will stand a better chance of being taken onto the books of a reputable agency. But in the beginning it will almost certainly be a waste of time for you to approach an agent.

However, if you would like to prove me wrong, names and addresses of agents can be found in *The Writer's Handbook*. Don't, in the first instance, send them your play. Just write to introduce yourself and to say what you have written. Outline your plans and ask if they would be interested in reading your work. They may then ask you to send one or two recent examples of your work. If they like what they see they will suggest a meeting to discuss the possibility of representing you. Should this happen, remember that you are entering into a relationship which should be mutually beneficial. Not only should the agent feel convinced that you are likely to earn her money, you should feel convinced that she understands your work and your aspirations and can commit herself to working hard to represent it to others. A very big and famous agency will be prestigious but, since you will probably be the least illustrious person they represent, this may not help you to get work. A smaller, more modest agency will probably give you more personal attention and support but may have less influence with theatres and other organisations.

It is important that the script you send out looks presentable. There is no need to waste money on expensive binding or fancy packaging but the text should be clear, clean and legible. Use a readable type-face, double spaced, and leave generous margins. If a script looks messy it will only act as a deterrent to a director who has so many others to choose from. Always send a brief accompanying letter and a stamped addressed envelope in which your play can be returned.

You may receive different advice elsewhere but I don't think that synopses, explanations, apologies, character notes or personal biographies help at all. They simply add to the pile of paperwork already cluttering up someone's desk. If you have a particularly impressive C.V. send it if you must, but it really isn't essential. The play is there to speak for itself. Never, never, never send the only copy of your script.

There is nothing (except the expense) to stop you from sending your play to several people simultaneously. If, by any chance, more than one theatre or director should take an interest in it, you will then be in the luxurious positon of being able to choose which one you prefer.

Now comes the worst bit — waiting. I wish I could tell you that you can send your play off and within two or three days you will get a polite acknowledgement. I wish I could say that, two to three weeks after this, you will receive a critical response to your script and that, within that space of time, you will know whether or not it has been accepted.

The reality is far more depressing. There are a few exemplary theatres which acknowledge scripts and give an indication of how long it might take them to read them. There are other theatres which manage to respond within three months, sending a reasoned and sympathetic criticism of your play if it is rejected.

But by far the most common response to your work is a deafening, baffling and hurtful silence. The Arts Council, The Writers' Guild and The Theatre Writers' Union have all in their time attempted to lay down a code of good practice for the treatment of scripts. All, it would seem, have failed. Theatres and their directors will sit on a script for months, even years, will fail to respond to letters, phone calls, threats of madness and mayhem.

Then, one day, just as you've forgotten that you ever wrote a play, a tattered and dog-eared object, ringed with coffee stains, looking as if birds have nested in it or beasts have nibbled at it, will arrive. It may be accompanied by a critical appraisal, or it may not. There may be an apology for the delay and a number of plausible if pathetic excuses, or there may not.

Of course, if your play has been accepted, all you will receive is a letter or even a phone call. In your excitement, all will be forgiven. If it has been rejected, the careless treatment of your work will only add to your sense of disappointment and failure.

Dealing with rejection is never easy, whether on a personal or professional level.

For a writer, rejection of your work, is a strange mixture of both. In order to write your play you have reached deep into parts of yourself normally left untouched; you have shared secrets, memories, dreams. You have laid bare your most private beliefs, fears and desires. You have probably made many personal sacrifices. You have invited scorn, disbelief and even, perhaps, accusations of madness. All this, you feel, would have been justified if your work had been accepted, if you had emerged triumphant wielding a contract, a cheque, performance dates. Every writer wants to be taken seriously. Every writer wants to take herself seriously; however secure we feel in ourselves, external approval, backed by the willingness to pay us the going rate for our work, is one recognised measure of acceptance in our society. However much we may believe that we write only for ourselves, for the sheer pleasure and fulfilment of it, there can be few of us who would not prefer acceptance to rejection.

But art is very much a matter of personal taste. Your play has been read by one or, at the most, two people. If it does not appeal to them, if it does not meet with their conscious or unconscious criteria of excellence or even acceptability, it doesn't mean that it is a bad play. It simply means that there is one person who doesn't like it. When you get your first rejection slip, allow yourself the natural grief at realising that not everyone sees your work as perfect. Try to absorb whatever criticism has been made and assess whether or not it contains a grain of truth. Expect a day or so of anger and disbelief, followed by a sense of insecurity about your work in general, and a deep feeling of negativity or depression. Then put the play in a big brown envelope and send it out again.

I think that women writers experience a particularly acute response when their work is rejected.

Writing anything requires great courage — finding your own voice and daring to use it, perhaps for the first time. You have explored aspects of feeling and experience hitherto undiscovered and unclaimed, demanding time and space in which to work in the midst of domestic duties or other responsibilities. All this has combined to create a very powerful and special experience. Now you seek some validation for your efforts and some recognition from outside.

More often than not you are, as ever, forced to submit your work to the decision of one man in authority. This raises problems on both sides. For your part there is the familiar anxiety attached to asking for 'daddy's' approval, the familiar pain when it is withheld. Where the work is essentially female in form or content, where it delves deep into a woman's psyche and experience, it will make strenuous and unfamiliar demands on any man who is required to respond to it. He may truthfully regard his response as objective, and may fully believe it to be so, but it will, in fact, be automatically filtered through his male consciousness. Because we are all so conditioned by patriarchy to accept the validity of the male viewpoint, a female analysis seems strange and incongruous, even to many women. It is not simply a question of subject matter but of your entire approach, your view of the world and your part in it.

There is no easy way of overcoming or counteracting this. I certainly wouldn't suggest that you modify what you write in order to accommodate the sensibilities of the establishment. But you may as well understand that you are operating under a severe handicap. Even if in the last few years there has been an upsurge of interest in women's writing there is still pitifully little space for the type of work which seriously challenges the status quo, which explores dark and dangerous territory. Women's work is acceptable, even fashionable, provided it doesn't go too far, ask too many questions, undermine too many assumptions.

There are, as always, exceptions. It is possible to find male directors who are very sensitive to women's writing but they are thin on the ground. And there are some excellent and courageous women directors who make a serious commitment to women's writing, indeed to ground-breaking new writing by men *and* women. Unfortunately, by their very commitment, they place themselves in a beleaguered position. They are constantly under intense pressure and might not always have as much time to devote to your work as they might ideally wish.

Again, it is useful to follow the work of such directors, to try to form an opinion as to who might take a special interest in what you have written. If you identify a director whose outlook seems to be in sympathy with your own it may be worth writing a personal letter, outlining why you believe your work might appeal.

We are all so used to coping with rejection that acceptance is almost more difficult to deal with. Instead of seeing your script returned in a brown paper envelope with a polite but cool letter you may receive a much more encouraging response. Your play has been accepted, a slot will be reserved for it in the forthcoming season. Can you make contact to discuss details of director, casting, etc . . . ?

You pick yourself up from the floor then panic sets in. There must be some mistake! Surely they mean someone else? Anyone who likes my play needs his brains tested. What if nobody comes to see it? Relax. Take a deep breath. Of course, you will feel a strange mixture of excitement and apprehension. You are about to enter the arena — your play is soon to become public property.

If you have no agent you will have to cope personally with the financial aspects involved in having a play accepted. How much should a theatre pay for the privilege of performing your work? What are royalties and how much will they amount to? If you feel unable to negotiate this aspect of things on your own you should seek advice from the Theatre Writers' Union or the Writers' Guild.

These professional organisations exist, like any union, to offer support and protection to their members. Both have been involved for many years in negotiating fair wage deals and adequate remuneration for writers in the theatre. A list of current fees, as negotiated, is published by both unions.

If your play is to be produced on the fringe, payment will be at a lower level. In some modest venues there will be no fee as such; instead you will be offered royalties (probably at 7½–10%). Royalties are a percentage of the box-office takings so at a small venue, where the seating can only accommodate 60–80 and the play is to run for a limited period, payment will not amount to a great deal. 'Profit-share' is a system where the writer, director and actors are paid nothing at all until the end of the run. Expenses such as publicity are then deducted from the box-office takings and the remaining sum is divided amongst all concerned. This will not be a fortune.

If a major theatre wants your work then you are in a better position. Arts Council schemes such as the Royalty Supplement Guarantee exist to ensure fair remuneration for a writer in the professional theatre. It is up to you to weigh up the situation and decide whether you are being offered a good contract or not.

If you know who you would like to direct your play discuss this with the theatre management. A small fringe venue may not have resident directors and will welcome your suggestions. A larger theatre may have staff directors so your options will probably be limited. Meet with the prospective director and listen to her ideas. Does she have a good understanding of the text? Is she broadly in sympathy with your aims? Some directors are very concerned to serve the text and will be happy to involve you in a serious way. Others have strong and idiosyncratic ideas which they intend to impose on your play. Don't agree to anything which you find repugnant, misconceived or inappropriate.

The director must consult you about casting and a major theatre should be willing to discuss your preferences. Remember that all theatres have tight budgets so be realistic. Where actors are to be employed on a profit-share basis you will have to accept that not everyone is prepared to offer their services in this way.

The design for your play will be an important aspect of the production. A model of the intended design will probably be presented to you by the designer before rehearsals begin. Don't expect a literal translation of your stage directions. A designer works creatively to interpret what she feels is your intention, using her knowledge of the effect of colour, stage lighting, etc. Stage design employs a great deal of *trompe l'oeil*, skilfully creating convincing pictures for the audience. Objects on the set may be used symbolically and the designer may decide against a naturalistic representation in favour of a more surreal or metaphorical approach. But if, after all your attempts to understand how the design works, it still doesn't feel right, then you must say so and make some alternative suggestions.

Before rehearsals begin you and the director should discuss what role you are to play in the process. The Writers' Guild clearly stipulates that a playwright has the right to attend as many rehearsals as she wishes. You may feel you'd like to be there all day and every day but very few directors will enjoy this and it can have a very inhibiting effect. The director needs to feel trusted, to be allowed some time to explore and develop her own ideas. If you insist on supervising her every move she will have no creative space in which to operate. Probably the best arrangement is for you to be there at the start in order to see the process under way. This will give you the opportunity to feel sure that things are progressing along the right lines. It will also give the director and actors a chance to ask you questions. Then it might be better for you to disappear for a while, returning in the middle of rehearsals for a couple of days. By that time certain problems may have emerged. The director may be considering cuts and changes which she will ask you to approve or implement. If all is running smoothly you can now disappear till the last two or three days when you can return to reassure yourself that all is going well.

There are harmonious rehearsal periods and exciting rehearsal periods. There are rehearsals where the whole process runs smoothly and all is beautifully under control. There are also rehearsal periods where everyone becomes quite worried that the play won't work. If things aren't progressing well discuss your misgivings in private with the director. Bringing a new play to the stage is always a difficult process. The text is fluid and the characters must be created for the first time. Writers who storm out of rehearsals do more harm than good, undermining the confidence of all concerned. There are very few problems, however severe, which can't be solved by frank discussion, by listening to different viewpoints, by a willingness to be open to the suggestions of others.

Sometimes gaping holes will open up in the text. Be prepared to respond quickly with emergency surgery. A good director shouldn't need to bully a writer. Actors may suggest changes but should channel their comments through the director. Don't submit to pressure. Although flexibility is at a premium, don't agree to any changes you don't understand or see the need for. Ask for time to consider, look calmly and closely at the text and, if you still feel it doesn't need to be changed, ask the director to discuss new ways of making it work.

The writer in rehearsal has to steer a difficult middle path between being too accommodating and being too rigid. Letting go of your play is an integral part of seeing it through rehearsal to production. If you hold on to your text too fiercely you will be putting your work at a disadvantage.

If director and actors have no confidence in what they have to interpret to the audience then they cannot present the best possible account of what you have written. The audience does not have the text to look at, they can only experience the play as performed. Though they may later read it in print their main impression comes from what they see on the stage.

On the other hand, you still have your personal vision to consider. You, above everyone, know what you mean. A good rehearsal process is one in which writer and director are in tune, working together to lift the play off the page.

The first night comes. You sit, undetected, in the audience. You experience a strange mixture of strong emotions. You feel very vulnerable . . . terrified that the audience won't like your play, won't understand or appreciate it. But you are also proud and excited. The weeks of isolation, the exhausting work, the uncertainty, the waiting are all in the past if not forgotten. The theatre is full of people who have come specially to see something that you have created. The actors are dressed and made up, ready to enact your story. The house lights go down; the stage lights come up. The play begins.

Sitting in the auditorium you will probably be too nervous to watch the stage — except when a piece of scenery threatens to fall or an actor forgets a line. Instead you will watch the audience, hungry for their reaction, dying a thousand deaths if there is just one bored or baffled face, delirious and disbelieving when anyone laughs at your jokes or cries at the sad bits.

Afterwards there is the response of friends and strangers and the cruelty of critics. Some will have liked the play, others won't. Some will have understood it well, empathised with your viewpoint. Others will have almost wilfully misunderstood every word. Exposed once more to the judgement of those whose view of the world may be vastly different from your own, you will feel very fragile. There are plays — very rarely — which everyone loves. You feel endorsed, valued, vindicated. There are plays which everyone hates. You feel mystified, cut to ribbons, angry, defensive.

You will have to learn to interpret the reaction of both audience and critics as objectively as you can, though this will never be easy. Are there places where the text lacks clarity? Is that, perhaps, why so many people failed to understand what you were saying? Are there any passages that need cutting? Is that, perhaps, why people looked in danger of nodding off?

It is always unwise to ignore audience reaction but it is equally unwise to allow it to destroy you. Instead, learn from it, absorb it, use it to your advantage, then let it go. Opportunities for discussion with members of the audience will be revealing or challenging and an honest and constructive response will leave you better prepared when you start work on your next play.

Writers always claim that they don't read the critics. What this means is that they only read them when they are complimentary.

There are, of course, good critics and bad critics. A good critic makes an honest attempt to understand your intention and to evaluate to what extent you have fulfilled it. He will suggest how your work may be improved in theatrical terms. He will point out to a prospective audience what they will enjoy in your play and help to clarify what seems difficult or obscure. A good critic will set your play in some kind of wider context and compare it with other contemporary work. He will also distinguish between genuine failures of the text and inadequacies in performance or interpretation.

A bad critic will pull to pieces what he can't immediately understand, will destroy all faith in what you have to say and poke fun at your inadequacies. He will be incapable of seeing beyond his personal prejudices and preconceptions.

Theatre critics aren't gods though they may assume the power to make or break a writer. They deserve only as much respect as the integrity of their work commands. Irving Wardle once condemned my play *People for Dinner* as "fit only for the waste disposal unit", thus ensuring that no one came to see it for themselves. David Harrison of the *Bristol Evening Post* kindly phoned to apologise to me when his editor cut his review of *Watching Foxes,* which made it more harshly critical than he had intended.

If your play is to be produced you may want to consider publication. I don't advise publication of an unperformed play because it is impossible to make hard and fast decisions about a text before it has been through the complete process of rehearsal and performance. Even after a premiere production you may still wish to make further changes before offering it for publication.

It is not easy to get a play published. Few publishers are interested in unknown or little known playwrights. But publication is valuable because it brings your work to a wider public and keeps it in circulation. *The Writer's Handbook* contains a list of drama publishers. Write to see if they are interested before sending the script.

Whether or not your play has been accepted for production or publication you should be feeling very proud and satisfied. You have worked alone with little support and no guarantee of success. You have struggled with self-doubt and insecurity, with technical problems and practical difficulties. And you have got there. You have completed an original piece of work to your own satisfaction.

Once you used to say: "I've always wanted to write but . . ."

Now you have proved to yourself that you *can* write. You have overcome all the obstacles, both external and internal . . . and you *have* written a play.

The Real Business of Writing

Now that you have gone through the difficult process of writing a play and the equally difficult process of seeking a response to what you have written, you are probably asking yourself: "What next?".

If you have had positive feedback to your work or, better still, have been offered either a production or a reading, you are probably already immersed in your next project.

Positive endorsement is the best encouragement any writer can have to continue writing. If the response to your work is good you will feel energised and excited at the prospect of writing something new. However much you may protest that you write simply for pleasure, or for personal satisfaction, it is extraordinary how crucial the response of others is to one's sense of worth as a writer. And if others fail to respond it will seem like a challenge not only to your basic skills but also to your personal values and philosophy.

If you have experienced rejection, adverse criticism or, worst of all, a total lack of interest in what you have written, you will have to fight hard against profound feelings of self-doubt before you can embark on a new piece of work.

To help overcome this it may be helpful to look on early pieces of work as a sort of rigorous apprenticeship, an opportunity to learn and practise unfamiliar skills. This will at least make you a little more philosophical about rejection and give you sufficient motivation to carry on.

Students sometimes ask me: "Am I a writer"? or "Will I ever be a *real* writer?" My answer is that the only difference between a real writer and someone who is flirting with the idea is that a real writer writes: she does it, continues to do it, finds sufficient strength, time, self-discipline, energy and motivation and goes on writing in spite of all the setbacks, personal difficulties, frustrations and, yes, rejection.

Real writers are probably driven to write by a compulsion so strong that no obstacle can stand in their way. They write more in hope than expectation and they carry on writing even when they achieve no recognition. Of course they know that their skills will improve with practice, that bit by bit they will learn more about their trade, but they don't write because they think it is a good way to earn a living. They write because they have no choice.

I am still in touch with many of the women who attended the two 'Made in Wales' workshops.

Two of the plays which came out of the first workshop — *Burd Mary* by Jane Buckler and *The Consecrator* by Charmian Savill — were given full productions by 'Made in Wales', as was *Echo Lady*, by Helen Gwyn, a product of the second workshop. Four of the plays had a rehearsed reading. Anne Challenor (whose play had provoked much interest but had no public production or reading) and Jane Buckler both embarked on government Enterprise schemes following the workshop, using the small but steady income to buy themselves time in which to continue to write.

In fact, most of the women are still writing, even if they feel that they cannot devote all their time to it. Marie, Gill, Katherine and Iris, who all came to the second workshop, have continued to meet on a regular basis, offering each other support and encouragement. All are either writing new plays or planning to do so.

Perhaps you are even wondering whether it might be possible to make a living from writing for the theatre. The answer is that it is possible but it's certainly not easy.

A few well-known and well-established playwrights may support a family, a mortgage, an expensive car, holidays abroad and still have money in the bank. Most professional writers tell a very different story. It's a hand-to-mouth existence; there's no career structure, no security and almost certainly no crock of gold at the foot of the rainbow. Nevertheless, at least there *is* a rainbow, which is more than you can say for most professions.

It's hard to imagine a job which would bring more freedom, a greater sense of autonomy, more flexibility, more potential for self-expression. There are also many fringe benefits.

I don't sit in a smoke-filled office or watch the clock on a factory floor. I can go for a walk, have a picnic, sleep or swim whenever I feel like it. I have no bosses, no working hours, no rules to obey. But neither do I have an official lunch break, luncheon vouchers, a set holiday, company pension or a regular pay packet. Instead I have hard deadlines to meet, bills to pay, and only my own imagination to rely on.

Of course, there are perfectly feasible compromises. You could make a serious commitment to writing whilst earning enough to meet your basic requirements from part-time employment. If writing is your top priority you could learn to live more simply in order to spend less.

You have the choice. But if you are someone who likes everything to be certain, with no room for shocks or surprises, then don't give up your day job. Writing as a profession is probably not for you.

On the positive side there are genuine opportunities for new writers who have one or two pieces of work to their credit. Small theatre companies are happy to commission writers relatively new to the profession, often to work on a devised play. In this process the writer works together with actors and directors to produce a script through discussion, improvisation and collaboration.

Many small-scale community plays are now being produced, largely as a result of the initiative set in motion by Ann Jellicoe and the Colway Theatre Trust. If such a play is planned in your area it may provide you with a rare chance to work boldly on a vast canvas, drawing on the resources of a large cast and local talent in the field of music or design. Such plays are not easy to write, even for an experienced writer, but if your local connections give you the opportunity then it could prove an exciting challenge.

A writers' workshop can offer a great deal of support and encouragement. However, the danger is that it can also develop into a cosy mutual admiration society, where genuine criticism is taboo and nobody dares overstep the mark. A good workshop will create a vibrant and questioning atmosphere. There will be genuine dialogue; members will constantly provoke and challenge each other thus pushing back the boundaries of their work.

But, when all is said and done, the only reason you will write and keep on writing is because you must, because you believe it is something worth doing and because you feel you may have something of value to say.

However many workshops you attend, organisations you join or books you read, the real work will always have to be done in isolation. Whoever or whatever you know, the most demanding and passionate relationship a writer ever has is with the blank sheet of paper.

We live in a time of ugliness and poverty, of dwindling resources and fierce competition for what little remains. Yet the very times we live in make it imperative that there are those who are determined to speak and to keep on speaking.

Perhaps you believe, as I do, that the theatre is one of the few remaining places where ordinary people can open themselves up to the extraordinary possibilities that are inherent in the universe and in every one of us. Where we can still experience pain, pleasure, beauty and poetry, not filtered through a screen, but living and breathing before our eyes.

Where we can remember not only what we are, but also what we might be.

And so you will write. And keep on writing. With integrity and commitment and a passionate belief that there is important work to be done.

****

May any merit which may result from the publication of this book go to the long life of my teacher, Ven. Geshé Damchö Yonten, and the happiness of all beings.

Notes

page 15

The Theatre Writers' Union, c/o The Actor's Centre, 4 Chenies Street, London WC1 7EP. Tel: 071 631 3619.

This is an organisation "open to any writer who has written a play or similar work for live performance." The following are the stated objectives of the Union: "To organise and represent all writers of theatre plays and other similar works for live performance and to improve pay, conditions and opportunities for union members."

The TWU also organises readings of new work by members and runs weekend workshops.

Playwrights: An Endangered Species (TWU, 1982).

Playwrights: A Species Still Endangered? (TWU, 1987).

page 18

Towards a Poor Theatre: Jerzy Grotowski (Eyre Methuen, 1976).

Jerzy Grotowski founded the Theatre Laboratory in Poland in 1959. Peter Brook described this as "perhaps the only avant-garde theatre whose poverty is not a drawback . . . . In his theatre there is absolute concentration by a small group and unlimited time." The Theatre Laboratory later attained the status of 'Institute for Research into Acting' and was not a theatre in the usual sense of the word but devoted to research into the art of theatre and the art of the actor.

page 18

The Empty Space: Peter Brook (Penguin, 1968).

Peter Brook is a legendary and often controversial theatre director. After memorable productions of classics such as *A Midsummer Night's Dream, King Lear* and the *Marat/Sade* for the Royal Shakespeare Company in the

1960's he left England to work in Paris, where he helped to set up the Centre for Theatre Research in 1970. Brook and his international company have since travelled widely to investigate the possibilities and origins of theatre. His work has taken him among African tribes and into a lengthy exploration of Indian myth and legend. His production of the *Mahabharata*, the fruit of ten years' intensive work, was produced in Britain in 1989 and subsequently adapted for television.

page 21

Bertolt Brecht: Marxist playwright and poet. As originator of the terms 'epic theatre' and the 'alienation effect' his influence is still widely felt in European theatre. After fleeing Nazi Germany he lived for a while in Hollywood but returned to East Berlin in 1948 to form The Berliner Ensemble, a theatre still devoted to the performance of his plays.

page 21

Community Plays: How to Put Them On: Ann Jellicoe (Methuen, 1987).

page 50

Research for Writers: Ann Hoffmann (Black, 1986).

page 51

The Public Record Office, Ruskin Avenue, Kew, Richmond, Surrey TW9 4DU. Tel: 081 876 3444. Some records have been retained at the original offices in Chancery Lane, London WC2A 1LR. Tel: 071 405 0741. Readers' tickets (valid for several years) or temporary tickets are obtainable at both.

page 57

Writers' and Artists' Yearbook (Black)

This directory is published annually and contains information on everything from markets for plays to the law of copyright.

page 138

The British Alternative Theatre Directory: Edited by Catherine Itzin (John Offord, annually from 1979–86). 1987 edition edited and published by Robert Conway and David McGillivray.

The British Alternative Theatre Directory: Directory of Playwrights, Directors and Designers: Edited by Catherine Itzin (John Offord, 1986).

page 138

The Writer's Handbook: Edited by Barry Turner (Macmillan/PEN, 1989).

An excellent and comprehensive reference book, with sections on theatre producers, agents and publishers, prizes, grants, etc.

page 143

The Writers' Guild of Great Britain, 430 Edgware Road, London W2 1EH. Tel: 071 723 8074

The Guild is a trade union representing writers in film, radio, TV and publishing.

page 144

The Royalty Supplement Guarantee

This is designed to supplement low income from royalties and to ensure a minimum sum to the writer.

The Arts Council have other schemes to help writers. Pamphlets may be obtained from: The Arts Council of Great Britain, 105 Piccadilly, London W1V 0AV. Tel: 071 629 9495.

Further Reading

Playwrights' Progress: Patterns of Postwar British Drama: Colin Chambers and Mike Prior (Amber Lane Press, 1987)

British Theatre Directory (John Offord)

The Penguin Dictionary of the Theatre: Edited by John Russell Taylor

A Better Direction: A national enquiry into the training of directors: Kenneth Rea (Calouste Gulbenkian Foundation, 1989)

Understudies: Theatre and Sexual Politics: Michelene Wandor (Eyre Methuen, 1981)

Q What do the following have in common:
Steven Berkoff · Michael Burrell ·
Anton Chekhov · Brian Clark ·
Barry Collins · Eduardo de Filippo ·
Keith Dewhurst · Nell Dunn ·
Charles Dyer · Rainer Werner Fassbinder ·
Donald Freed · Maxim Gorky ·
Richard Harris · Ronald Harwood ·
Franz Kafka · Roy Kift · Hanif Kureishi ·
Bob Larbey · Tony Marchant ·
Sean Mathias · Mark Medoff ·
Julian Mitchell · Mary O'Malley ·
Caryl Phillips · Manuel Puig ·
James Saunders · Anthony Shaffer ·
Martin Sherman · August Strindberg ·
Peter Terson · Heidi Thomas ·
Brian Thompson · John Wain ·
Hugh Whitemore · Snoo Wilson ·
David Wood · Sheila Yeger ?

A They're all playwrights, silly!

Q But what *sort* of playwrights?

———————➤

A   Amber Lane Playwrights, of course . . . .

Find out what you're missing out on by writing or phoning for a copy of our free catalogue.

AMBER LANE PRESS
Church Street, Charlbury, Oxford OX7 3PR.
(0608) 810024